My Spiritual Gifts

Including a Personal Inventory

A Guide for Youth

Kenneth Cain Kinghorn

Emeth Press

My Spiritual Gifts,
Including a Personal Inventory
Copyright © 2006 by Kenneth Cain Kinghorn
Printed in the United States of America on acid-free paper

All rights reserved. No part of this book may be reproduced, or stored in a retrieval system or transmitted in any form or by any means, electronic, mechanical, photocopying, recording, scanning or otherwise, except as permitted by the 1976 United States Copyright Act, or with the prior written permission of Emeth Press. Requests for permission should be addressed to: Emeth Press, P. O. Box 23961, Lexington, KY 40523-3961. http://www.emethpress.com

Library of Congress Control Number 2005930734

ISBN 978-0-9755435-8-0

Cover artwork (dove) by Richard Douglas
Graphics are used by permission:
www.christart.com, pp. 7, 11 (top right column), 13, 17 (bottom right column), 23, 24, 26 (right column), 28, 29, 30 (right column), 32 (top columns), 53, 54 (left column), 58, 66, 68, 73 (right column), 75 (left column), 76, 79, 81 (right column), 82, 97.
www.faithclipart.com, pp. 22, 26 (left column), 32 (bottom left column), 50, 54 (right column), 55.

Unless otherwise noted, all Scripture quotations are from the New Revised Standard Version Bible, copyright 1989, by the Division of Christian Education of the National Council of the Churches of Christ in the U.S.A. Used by permission. All rights reserved.

Scripture quotations marked (NLT) are taken from the *Holy Bible*, New Living Translation, copyright © 1996. Used by permission of Tyndale House Publishers, Inc., Wheaton, Illinois 60189. All rights reserved.

Scripture quotations marked (Message) are taken from *The Message* by Eugene H. Peterson, copyright © 1993, 1994, 1995, 1996, 2000, 2001, 2002. Used by permission of NavPress Publishing Group. All rights reserved

To My Students, Past and Present

Content

About this Book..7

1. Daring to Dream..11

2. Dispelling the Haze...21

3. Detecting the Treasure..29

4. Discerning the Distinctions..59

5. Directing the Focus..67

6. Discovering the Prize...81

About the Author..101

About This Book

Being a Christian is not so much about what we do for God as what God does for us. We need to know that Jesus came into the world not with a demand, but with an offer (John 3:17). He told us that he came that we may have life, and "have it to the full" (John 10:10).

An important part of the complete life Jesus promised you includes finding and using your spiritual gifts. So, the following pages are about you and the supernatural spiritual gifts that Christ gives to us all—the strongest of us and the weakest of us.

Your journey into adulthood will come sooner than you can imagine. It's important for teens to stand on solid ground and choose wisely as they prepare for life later on. Becoming grounded in Jesus Christ and knowing how he has gifted you will help you get ready for your march toward marriage, mission, and ministry.

Suppose a developer wants tree-lined streets in his new subdivision. Looking ahead, it's important that he plant the trees, and choose the kind of trees he wants to beautify the streets. Either failing to plant the trees or choosing junk trees won't bring the wished-for results. Good planning and right action make a world of difference.

We have only one life to live, and we want it to be a good one—the greatest one possible. Our best preparation for the future is first to know Jesus Christ, and second to discover and make the most of both our natural talents and supernatural gifts.

> *We have only one life to live, and we want it to be a good one— the greatest one possible.*

This book is about understanding, discovering, and using the divine gifts of the Holy Spirit. This adventure can lead to one of the most exciting and important breakthroughs of your life.

You've probably seen more surveys, polls, and examinations

than you can count. Medical checkups to assess your health, dental probes to test your teeth, psychological inventories to learn your personality type, and written surveys to measure your academic potential. All these kinds of assessments are useful, and they can even be enjoyable.

This book is about another part of your life—your spiritual makeup. In short, this book seeks several goals. It aims to:

- Identify the New Testament gifts of the Holy Spirit;
- Explain the spiritual gifts;
- Clear up some common confusions about the Holy Spirit's gifts;
- Summarize the biblical guidelines for understanding and exercising spiritual gifts;
- Help you discover the spiritual gifts God has given you.

This knowledge can change your life radically.

This book neither removes nor adds to the lists of gifts St. Paul gave us. We'll not look at the gifts of the Holy Spirit from any particular denominational standpoint. The Bible speaks for itself.

My aim is to unite Christians, not drive them apart; add to our dependence on Christ, not lesson it; encourage more variety among Christians, not more sameness; increase humility, not pride.

As you discover and enter fully into God's will for your life, you will begin to unlock your potential and you'll find the marvelous future he has designed for you. God wants you to live productively and creatively, storing up treasures in heaven, just as Jesus advised (Matt. 6:20). In doing so, one day you will gain the everlasting rewards God prepares for those who live a well-spent life. By God's grace, such a life is yours for the asking.

An Exercise for Dreamers

Asking Myself a Question

Before you dig into these pages, let's look at an important question, which you alone can answer. In some ways, it's a simple question, and in other ways it's one of the most far-reaching questions any teen can ask herself or himself. Your response can determine the nature and quality of your entire life. For that matter, it can affect your existence in eternity.

Here's the question:

What do I want most from now until I'm forty years old?

Look at the following possibilities. Circle only one letter (A-F).

A. Make a ton of money and retire early.
B. Break into the headlines as a sports hero, music star, actor, or governor of the State.
C. Discover my unique, God-given potential, and trust that God has a plan for my life better than any plan I could dream.
D. Invent a useful tool or machine that will make life easier for others and make me famous.
E. Marry the most handsome guy or gorgeous girl in the entire State.
F. Sponge off others and do as little as possible.

Here are two suggested ways to process your answer...

Imagine you gained your preferred choice of life by the age of forty. Write three or four sentences about what you think your life would be like when you reach 80 years of age. Think about the alternate answers, based on a different lifetime dream. Did you make the right choice? Write a short prayer, no longer than a paragraph, talking to God about what selection you marked and why you marked it. Ask him to show you what dream of life at 40 he wants you to imagine.

_____

_____

_____

_____

OR

Discuss with a small group, containing both guys and gals, what you think your life would be like when you become 80 years old, based on your answer to the question. Discuss the pros and cons of the alternate answers.

1
Daring to Dream

We need God's power in our lives as much as TV's need electricity and cars need gas. True, God created us in his image and likeness, and our human potential is amazing. Yet, God did not make us to live apart from him. Jesus compared us to the branches of a vine. He said, "Just as the branch cannot bear fruit by itself unless it abides in the vine, neither can you unless you abide in me....Apart from me you can do nothing" (John 15:4-7). Although branches themselves lack the power to produce fruit, when connected to the vine they can bless the world. So can we, but only as God's power flows through our lives. Compared with God, we are as dumb as door knobs and as helpless as babies. To be effective we need God's power.

One of the important ways God's power works in us is by the gifts of the Holy Spirit. Spiritual gifts give us the power 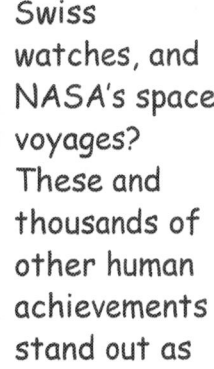 to become more and do more than we might dare to dream. Without God's work in our lives, we have limited wisdom and few abilities. To be sure, natural talents can sometimes lead to remarkable accomplishments. Who can deny the human genius we see in Egypt's pyramids, the *Encyclopaedia Britannica*, nineteenth-century Swiss watches, and NASA's space voyages? These and thousands of other human achievements stand out as impressive human triumphs. Yet, eventually all our successes will fade

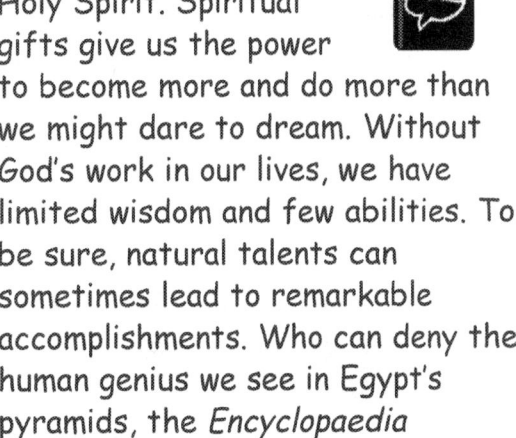

away and disappear from the earth. Only Spirit-inspired works for God will continue forever. God has a divine plan for each of us, which includes eternal outcomes and rewards. Much of this plan calls for knowing and using our spiritual gifts.

One day, each of us will give an account to God for the way we've managed and used all that God has given us. This is called stewardship. Although we do not earn heaven by good works, we will receive everlasting rewards for faithful service. Scripture says we will have all the secrets of our lives revealed at the final day of judgment before Christ (2 Cor. 5:10). We are wise to "store up for ourselves treasures in heaven, where neither moth nor rust consumes and where thieves do not break in and steal" (Matt. 5:20). Jesus promised that he will "come with his angels in the glory of the Father, and then he will repay everyone for what has been done" (Matt. 16:27).

If all followers of Christ discovered their spiritual gifts, developed them, and used them, as Christians did in the Book of Acts, they would "turn the world upside down" (Acts 17:6). Living as God intends, we find joy and fulfillment in our daily lives. Jesus promised to give us a full life (John 10:10), and the gifts of the Holy Spirit are a part of this plan (Heb. 2:4; 1 Peter 4:10). God wants us to spring into each new day with anticipation, hope, and confidence that God is working in and through us to make a difference that lasts forever.

Yet, millions of Christians remain unaware of their spiritual gifts. They haven't yet tapped into the enormous treasures that God has for them. At the finish of such half-empty lives, people can only look back with regret. They will realize they have spent their time and energy on things of very little lasting value.

Lukewarm discipleship causes much important Christian work to remain incomplete. Half-filled Christians seem powerless to turn back the untold heartache that blankets the earth. Today, concerned observers of modern culture are alarmed about the world's careless race toward Armageddon.

The fault does not lie in the lack of God's power to help his servants move the world in the right direction. God gives us awesome power and authority for ministry and service. Yet, careless Christians fail to understand or use God's marvelous gifts. To speak bluntly, some who profess to follow

Christ resist, ignore and hurt the Holy Spirit (Eph. 4:30; 1 Thess. 5:19).

God's gifts are too valuable to overlook and neglect. St. Paul reminds us that Christians are temples of the Holy Spirit, who gives us power to glorify God in our bodies (1 Cor. 16:19-20). To use a comparison of Jesus, some Christians have allowed shallow soil and choking weeds to smother the good seed of God's word in their lives (Matt. 13:24-30). If they once bore fruit, they seem now to have lost their enthusiasm. The biblical remedy for a lazy life is to "rekindle the gift of God that is within you...for God did not give us a spirit of cowardice, but rather a spirit of power and of love and of self-discipline" (2 Tim. 1:7).

If one plans to build a house on a vacant lot, it's necessary to clear tree stumps, dynamite the boulders, and cart off the rubble. Sometimes building sites need light raking, and sometimes they benefit from heavy bulldozing. Also, before building a house it's necessary to measure the building site, lay out a solid foundation, and understand how best to use tools and building materials. If building a house calls for knowledge and planning, so does building a life.

At least three obstacles can keep us from discovering and using the spiritual gifts God has given us. Let's look at these joy-robbing, fruit-killing, regret-inducing obstacles. We can clear the ground, catch a vision of something better, and dare to dream of a fruitful and rewarding life.

1. Lack of Knowledge

The first boulder we often need to remove is our ignorance and lack of understanding.

An ancient legend tells the story of a hungry beggar who  spotted a group of travelers crossing the desert, led by a wealthy rice merchant.

The hungry beggar pleaded with the merchant for rice. "I must have rice or I will die, and my family as well," the starving pauper groaned.

Touched with pity, the rice merchant asked, "How much do you need? I will give you all the rice you want for yourself and for your family."

The beggar asked for one hundred grains of rice, which the kind business man cheerfully gave him.

After the merchant's caravan left, the beggar's friends said, "Why did you ask for only one hundred grains? We can hardly believe you requested such a small amount! The man offered to give you all the rice you asked for."

The surprised beggar replied, "Tell me, is there a number greater than one hundred?"

Many Christians seem uninformed about God's vast power, plan, and provisions. Their ignorance of spiritual gifts blocks them from experiencing and using these priceless benefits.

If someone in a remote jungle does not know the meaning of the alphabet, that person cannot imagine the existence of books, the delights of reading, and the thrill of discovering more knowledge. If we do not know about spiritual gifts, we suffer under a huge handicap. St. Paul wrote, "Now concerning spiritual gifts, brothers and sisters, I do not want you to be uninformed....Now there are varieties of gifts, but the same Spirit, and there are varieties of services, but the same Lord, and there are varieties of activities, but it is the same God who activates all of them in everyone" (1 Cor. 12:1).

If it's possible to be unaware of our natural talents, we can also be ignorant of our spiritual gifts. People can have talents for carpentry, farming, poetry, mechanics, landscape design, art, or music. Yet, they sometimes remain unaware that these promising abilities lie hidden within them.

Talented people may never imagine themselves building a house, developing a garden, writing a poem, creating with their hands, painting a picture, or learning to sing or play a musical instrument. They live their lives without discovering the beauty they could create, the benefits they could give, the joy they could experience. If this fact is true in the natural world, it's also true in the spiritual world.

If a contractor were ignorant of electricity, he would not know the possibilities of its power. He would not likely think beyond using hand tools. If a baker knew nothing about yeast or salt, her bread-baking abilities would suffer seriously. St. Paul said that many "are darkened in

> "My people perish for lack of knowledge" (Hosea 4:6)

their understanding, alienated from the life of God because of their ignorance." Many people know little about spiritual gifts, and their lack of understanding keeps them from experiencing the Holy Spirit's wonderful blessings. The lack of knowledge settles as a dense fog that clouds our vision.

Happily, we do not have to live in ignorance. The Book of Proverbs trumpets one of God's most stirring promises: "If you call out for insight and cry aloud for understanding, and if you look for it as for silver and search for it as for hidden treasure, then you will understand... and find the knowledge of God. For the Lord gives wisdom, and from his mouth come knowledge and understanding."

Jesus said if we sincerely hunger for spiritual truth he will give it to us. In every instance in the Bible when someone asked God for understanding, he provided it. Our divine Creator delights to reveal himself, his truth, and his gifts. He is not far away, and our seeking always leads to our finding.

Jesus promised, "Ask, and it will be given you; search, and you will find; knock, and the door will be opened for you. For everyone who asks receives, and everyone who searches finds, and for everyone who knocks, the door will be opened" (Matt. 7:7-8). Jesus also assured us that when we know the truth, the truth will make us free (John 8:32). Understanding and using our spiritual gifts are important parts of becoming what God intends for us to be and to do. With God's help, we can move beyond ignorance into understanding.

2. Neglect of God's Laws and Commands

A second obstacle blocking our spiritual progress is the willful neglect of God and his truth. Self-will compares to a stubborn tree stump that keeps

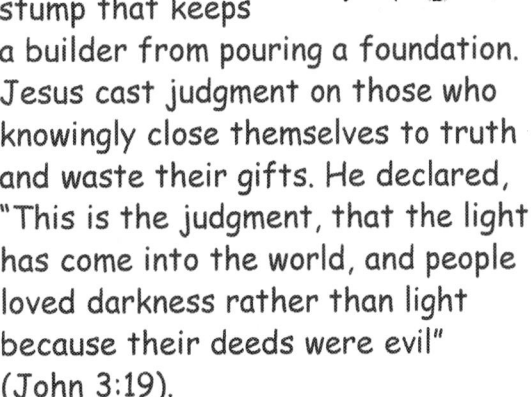

a builder from pouring a foundation. Jesus cast judgment on those who knowingly close themselves to truth and waste their gifts. He declared, "This is the judgment, that the light has come into the world, and people loved darkness rather than light because their deeds were evil" (John 3:19).

Simply put, some people prefer spiritual darkness to spiritual light because they want their own way more than God's way. That was Adam and Eve's biggest blunder. Putting self first was, and is, the root of all sin. Self-will and disobedience shattered Adam and Eve's communion with God, and the virus of spiritual corruption wormed its way into God's newly created world. Because they became fearful, the miserable couple "hid themselves from the presence of God."

We cannot build a house if we ignore or disobey the laws of physics, chemistry, or mathematics. It would be foolish for a contractor to expect gasoline to work in a diesel tractor or houses without foundations to stand in a swamp. It's equally reckless to believe we can fulfill God's purpose for our lives if we knowingly ignore his laws and promises.

St. Paul wrote about those who were "darkened in their understanding...because of the ignorance that is in them due to the hardening of their hearts." St. Augustine (354-430) said, "Sin is applying our energy in the wrong direction."

Jesus announced, "I am the light of the world. Whoever follows me will never walk in darkness but will have the light of life" (John 8:12). Jesus also taught an enduring principle: "Everyone then who hears these words of mine and acts on them will be like a wise man who built his house on rock" (Matt. 7:24). We miss out on a fulfilling life and eternal rewards when we knowingly disobey God by deliberately ignoring his will. Our Creator made us for something much better than putting ourselves first. It's better to dream God's dreams.

3. An Undisciplined Life

A third obstacle to spiritual progress is laziness. Careless habits creep like briars and thorns that get in the way of our building a house. The Book of Ecclesiastes says, "If a man is lazy, the rafters sag; if his hands are idle, the house leaks" (Eccles. 10:18 NIV). Those who would build a house must get out of bed, turn off the television, put on their gloves, and start working. They must show up regularly at the job site, keep their tools in good condition, follow the blueprint, and commit themselves to quality work. Those who yield to distractions, allow their tools to rust, or work carelessly cannot expect to build a good house.

Christians also must discipline themselves in the faithful use of their spiritual gifts. St. Paul encouraged Timothy, "Do your best to present yourself to God as one approved by him, a worker who has  no need to be ashamed" 2 Tim. 2:15). Left unused, our spiritual gifts lie hidden and inactive. If we were to store an acorn in a glass jar, the acorn could not develop into an oak tree. The acorn has all the potential to reach its promise, but unless it finds its home in God's good earth it cannot become a tree.

Regardless of what your spiritual gifts are, they will flourish only as you discover and use them. The writer of Hebrews encourages us: "We do not want you to become lazy, but to imitate those who through faith and patience inherit what has been promised" (Heb. 6:12, NIV).

Laziness is easy—that's why it's so common. However, few pursuits bring more satisfaction than a disciplined life. In 431 B.C. the philosopher Euripides said, "Do not consider painful what is good for you." Discussing spiritual gifts, Peter declared, "Like good stewards of the manifold grace of God, serve one another with whatever gift each of you has received" (1 Pet. 4:10).

Scripture teaches clearly, "It is required of stewards that they are found trustworthy" (1 Cor. 4:1-2). Faithful stewards are successful builders.

The poet Henry Wadsworth Longfellow (1807-1882) reminded us,

> Life is real. Life is earnest;
> And the grave is not its goal;
> "Dust thou art, to dust returnest,"
> Was not spoken of the soul.

We are citizens of eternity, and the stakes are too high to settle for anything less than God's best. Part of his plan for us includes making the most of our spiritual gifts.

To guide us in his way, God helps us overcome the pitfalls of ignorance, willful neglect, and lack of discipline. Scripture invites us to embrace God's wisdom, energy, and purpose. His plan is good, and it leads to a future finer than dreams.

Being Honest with Myself
(This is ONLY between me and God)

Circle the answer that most applies to me

As for religion in my life, I must honestly say...

1. I believe in the existence of God, but I'm not a true follower of Jesus Christ. I'm not ready to make that commitment. For now, there are other things more important to me.

2. I'd like to follow Christ, but I don't know how. Truthfully, no one has ever explained to me how to become a Christian. I think it's time I started a serious search for a personal knowledge of God and what the Bible says about Christian discipleship. *(Read again point one in this chapter).*

3. I'm a Christian, but I'm an "on-again-off-again" disciple. Lukewarm, to tell the truth. It's not that I've turned away from Christ, yet I'm not a growing Christian. Sometimes I overlook the Lord because other things get in the way of my relationship with him. I don't reject him, but I do neglect him. *(Read again point two in this chapter).*

4. I confess I'm lazy and undisciplined in my spiritual life. I can discipline myself in academics or sports, but not in religion. I've got to make up my mind whether I want to be a 50% Christian or a 100% Christian. *(Read again point three in this chapter).*

5. God knows I love him with all my heart. And the more I know him, the more I want to know him still better. I do fall short sometimes, but my deepest desire is to know him more clearly and follow him more closely..

Daring to Dream 19

Depending on which number you checked, write a personal prayer to God about your relationship to him. Be honest. There's no way we can hide anything from God or avoid having to answer to him one day.

_____
_____
_____
_____
_____
_____

Is your prayer a confession? Did you ask God for wisdom and guidance? Did you thank and praise Him? Did you ask Him to take control of your life? Your written prayer is not for anyone else to read. It's between you and God alone.

> "Is there any place I can go to avoid your Spirit?
> to be out of your sight?
> If I climb to the sky, you're there!
> If I go underground, you're there!
> If I flew on morning's wings
> to the far western horizon,
> You'd find me in a minute—
> you're already there waiting!
> Then I said to myself, "Oh, he even sees me in the dark!
> At night I'm immersed in the light!"
> It's a fact: darkness isn't dark to you,
> night and day, darkness and light,
> they're all the same to you.
> (Psalm 139:7-12, THE MESSAGE)

2
Dispelling the Haze

The New Testament does not give us a dictionary definition of the gifts of the Spirit. For that matter, the Bible doesn't contain formal essays about other important doctrines, such as the Trinity and baptism. Nonetheless, scripture clearly teaches these subjects and gives us plenty of information about them. Simply stated, the Bible is not a collection of formal essays. Rather, it is the story of how God revealed Himself in the history of the world, which reached its completion in the life, death, and resurrection of Jesus Christ and the sending of his Holy Spirit on the day of Pentecost.

Even if scripture does not contain an academic essay on spiritual gifts, it does reveal much about them. The New Testament lists the spiritual gifts and shows how they were used in the first century. Acts, for instance, gives us many examples of people using spiritual gifts. Also, Paul, Peter, and other New Testament apostles disclose important information about the subject.

The most often used New Testament word for spiritual gift is *charisma*. The plural form of the word is *charismata*. *Charisma* comes from the Greek word *charis*, which means "grace," "goodwill," "favor," or "loving kindness." So a spiritual gift is a favor or benefit one receives apart from human merit—a "gift of grace," or a "grace-gift."

Spiritual gifts are God-given abilities that the Holy Spirit imparts to Christians for service to

Christ and others. These *charismata* enable Christians to minister in extraordinary ways, beyond their natural abilities and human talents.

We can better understand spiritual gifts by grasping three principles:

- Spiritual gifts come from the Holy Spirit—not from the church, our pastor, our parents, or our personal determination. *"All [spiritual gifts] are activated by one and the same Spirit, who allots to each one individually just as the Spirit chooses"* (1 Cor. 12:11).

- Spiritual gifts are God-given abilities that help us to do more than our natural possibilities will allow. *"You will receive power when the Holy Spirit has come upon you; and you will be my witnesses"* (Acts 1:8).

- Spiritual gifts bring responsibilities for which God expects us to be faithful. *"Each of us will be accountable to God"* (2 Cor. 5:10).

The New Testament lists twenty spiritual gifts, and St. Paul gives them in four places. Christians sometimes discuss whether this list of New Testament gifts is complete, or whether there are others. Can we, or should we, add other spiritual gifts to these lists?

There *may* be gifts of the Holy Spirit other than those listed in the New Testament, but the New Testament writers do not record them. It is true that scripture speaks of such actions as hospitality, singing, and defending the faith against false teachers. These good works, however, are not spiritual gifts—they are *ministries* that depend on spiritual gifts.

The New Testament also speaks of those who died for their faith (martyrdom), of those who remained unmarried (permanent celibacy) for the sake of their ministry, of those who experience suffering and

persecution. These circumstances, however, do not qualify as spiritual gifts, although they call for special spiritual *graces* to deal with the challenges and opportunities we meet.

St. Paul writes about spiritual gifts in 1 Corinthians 12:4-6:

> Now there are varieties of gifts, but the same Spirit. And there are varieties of ministries, but the same Lord. And there are varieties of effects, but the same God who works all things in all persons.

Note that the apostle uses three nouns—varieties of **gifts**, varieties of **ministries**, and varieties of **effects**. We can infer that *gifts* flow through *ministries*, leading to *effects* (or *results*).

We should not *add* spiritual gifts to the New Testament lists without biblical support for doing so. Also, we should not *delete* spiritual gifts which the New Testament plainly records. Faithfulness to the New Testament is essential if we wish to avoid guesswork and speculation. Always, the Bible remains our final source of religious truth.

For centuries, God's people have confessed that God's word is a "lamp to our feet" and a "light to our path" (Psalm 119:105). Christians pray, "The unfolding of your words gives light; it gives understanding to the simple" (Psalm 119:130).

Luke wrote about the Christians in Berea: "Now these were nobler than those in Thessalonica, in that they received the word with all readiness of the mind, examining the Scriptures daily, whether these things were so. Many of them therefore believed" (Acts 17:11-12). Final judgments must agree with scripture.

St. Paul wrote the first-century Corinthians, quoting God's revelation in the Book of Isaiah: "I will destroy the wisdom of the wise, and the discernment of the discerning I will thwart" (1 Cor. 1:19). He continued, "We speak, not in words taught us by human wisdom but in words taught by the Spirit, expressing spiritual truths in spiritual words" (1 Cor. 2:13). John Wesley declared, "I am a Bible-bigot. I follow it in all things great and small." Wesley's reverence for the Bible echoes every Protestant creed, which all affirm the final authority of scripture.

We can clearly identify twenty spiritual gifts, because the New Testament specifically lists them. These gifts cover the full range of

Christian ministries. And if we focus our study on these spiritual gifts, we stand on solid biblical ground.

The Apostle Peter also discussed spiritual gifts, but he did not provide us with lists, as Paul did. Peter encourages us to glorify God by faithfully using the spiritual gifts God gives us. He wrote,

> Like good stewards of the varied grace of God, serve one another with whatever gift each of you has received. Whoever speaks must do so as one speaking the very words of God; whoever serves must do so with the strength that God supplies, so that God may be glorified in all things through Jesus Christ (1 Peter 4:10-11).

Instead of making a formal list of the spiritual gifts, Peter chose to write about two *categories* of gifts—*speaking* gifts and *action* gifts. Some vocal gifts—such as teaching—use words. Practical gifts—such as administration—involve action. Of course, the teacher should serve, and the administrator should speak. Even so, as Peter suggests, some gifts chiefly involve words and other gifts mainly call for deeds.

The Book of Hebrews also touches on spiritual gifts, but again without specifically listing them, as does St. Paul. The writer of Hebrews speaks of spiritual gifts as proof that God is active in the world: "God added his testimony by signs and wonders and various miracles, and by gifts of the Holy Spirit, distributed according to his will" (Heb. 2:4). Whatever gifts God gives us, by our using them "God is

glorified in all things through Jesus Christ."

The chart on the next page contains the spiritual gifts listed in St. Paul's four main New Testament passages dealing with this subject. There are still other places in the Bible that mention spiritual gifts, but in each case they speak of gifts listed in this chart.

St. Paul's Lists of the Gifts of the Spirit

Romans 12:6-8	1 Cor. 12:4-11	1 Cor. 12:28-30	Ephesians 4:11
Prophecy Teaching Serving Exhortation Giving Giving Aid Compassion	Prophecy Healing Working Miracles Tongues Interpretation of tongues Word of wisdom Word of knowledge Faith Discernment	Prophecy Teaching Healing Working Miracles Tongues Interpretation of tongues Apostleship Helps Administration	Prophecy Teaching Apostleship Evangelism Shepherding

"It is the one and only Spirit who distributes all these gifts. He alone decides which gift each person should have" (1 Cor. 12:11, *New Living Translation*).

The next chapter defines in detail each of the twenty New Testament gifts of the Holy Spirit. As you study these spiritual gifts, you'll better understand the variety of *charismata* God has given the church for our common good.

Even if you do not have a certain gift that you will read about, you can nevertheless deepen the quality of your life by understanding them.

For example, you may not have the gifts of giving, compassion, teaching, or administration. Yet, as you study these gifts you can bring the qualities of generosity, caring, sharing, and daring into your life. God can deepen and broaden your life with some of the qualities of the gifts you do not have. And you will be better able to recognize gifts in others and affirm them in their ministries.

You will also find that one or more of the spiritual gifts will resonate deeply within you. The Holy Spirit is helping you discover the special gift or gifts he has given you. Pay attention to your inner voice. The Holy Spirit is probably speaking to you and helping you identify your spiritual gift or gifts. God has watched over you since your birth, and he wants to show you the *charismata* he has given you.

An unknown poet wrote these encouraging lines:

> Whoso draws near to God, one step
> Through doubtings dim,
> God will advance a mile
> In blazing light to him.

The Holy Spirit enlightens our understanding of scripture. As its truths take root in our lives, we find that God is leading us into the blazing light of a future more splendid than the noonday sun.

TRUE CHRISTIANS WILL ONE DAY INHERIT FANTASTIC GLORY

Understanding the Spiritual Gifts
(A Group Activity)

Before the youth meeting, the leader or someone else needs to get twenty poster boards large enough for group viewing. Have someone print each spiritual gift in large letters on a different poster.

Each person should bring as many different versions of the Bible as possible—King James Version, Revised Standard Bible, New English Bible, Phillips translation, NIV Bible, The Message, etc. As many different versions as they can find. There are dozens of translations, of course. You could have a contest between the guys and girls to see which group brings the largest number of translations, and who brings the oldest Bible. (You could award a prize to someone bringing the oldest Bible).

Let the leader ask the group to turn first to Romans 12:6-8. This scripture contains seven spiritual gifts. The leader begins by displaying the first poster board (which has at the top "Prophecy"). Ask the group to consult the different versions of the Bible and call out how the spiritual gift translates in their version. Some spiritual gifts appear the same way in almost all the translations. In other cases, various versions of the Bible use different words to translate the spiritual gifts. On the poster board, have someone print neatly (in large letters) all the different biblical translations of the word Prophecy. Continue this procedure through each of the seven gifts in this first passage of scripture.

Then have the group turn to 1 Corinthians 12:4-11. That passage contains 9 spiritual gifts. Repeat the process—poster by poster, printing the assorted biblical translations of each spiritual gift.

The final two passages are 1 Corinthians 12:28-30 (nine gifts) and Ephesians 4:11 (five gifts). Many of the gifts appear in more than one of these scripture passages; some gifts appear in only one passage.

Group discussion can focus on the subtle shades of meanings of the various translations, while also recognizing that each translation points to the same spiritual gift.

The next chapter in this book describes each of the spiritual gifts.

> If parents love to give material gifts to their children, how much more does God love to give spiritual gifts to his children!

3

Detecting the Treasure

To define the spiritual gifts, we will not entirely rely on present-day meanings of words. Our dictionaries do not always reflect the scriptural and theological meanings of terms. The study of any biblical theme calls for the right method. This chapter relies on four principles of biblical interpretation:

- The meaning of the original New Testament words.
- The use of spiritual gifts in the New Testament church.
- The insights of the best thinkers in the Christian tradition.
- The experiences of Spirit-filled Christians.

We will define the *charismata* based on these classic Christian tests for truth. We will look at the spiritual gifts in the order they appear on the back cover of this book, or on page 25.

1. Prophecy

Applying the biblical revelation with clarity and power as light and truth for the present (Rom. 12:6)

The Greek word *propheteia* means to "speak forth," "speak openly," "preach God's message," "announce," or "make known." Chiefly, this New Testament word refers to proclaiming the mind and counsel of the Lord. The Old Testament prophets focused on God's promise and purpose of salvation, and the future coming of his Messiah and his kingdom. New

Testament prophecy focused on the centrality of Jesus Christ as fully God. St. Paul emphasized this truth: "For I handed on to you as of first importance what I in turn had received: that Christ died for our sins in accordance with the scriptures, and that he was buried, and that he was raised on the third day in accordance with the scriptures" (1 Cor. 15:3-4).

The apostle Peter describes this spiritual gift as "speaking the oracles of God." The gift of prophecy does not come from human origins or authority. It comes from God. The prophet Jeremiah wrote, "Then the LORD put out his hand and touched my mouth; and the LORD said to me, 'Now I have put my words in your mouth'" (Jer. 1:9).

In our time, the major purpose of this gift is not prediction of future events, but telling what God has done in Jesus Christ—not foretelling that something is going to happen, but  forth-telling or announcing what God has already done in human history.

The New Testament does contain a few instances of prophetic prediction. St. Paul, for instance, saw in advance a shipwreck, in which all would survive (Acts 27:10, 21-22). The gift of prophecy, however, refers mainly to declaring God's truths to specific people and places. We can define the gift of prophecy as enabling one to understand God's word and effectively apply it with extraordinary depth and power. God uses the gift of prophecy to teach, build up, encourage, and console (1 Cor. 14:3).

The New Testament warns against false prophets (*pseudoprophetes*) who come in sheep's clothing, but inwardly are "ravenous wolves" (Matt. 7:15). Jesus said, "Many false prophets will arise and lead many astray" (Matt. 24:11).

Scripture speaks of three kinds of false prophets: (1) Those who serve idols and worship false gods. (2) Those who falsely claim to receive messages and revelations from God. (3) Those former prophets who strayed from God and no longer obey or serve him.

We can know false prophets by their bad fruit or lack of good fruit. If a ministry does not glorify Christ and leads people away  from him, that ministry is false. Some of these false prophets may even appear to perform great signs and wonders (Matt. 24:24). Because their message flatters and gives enticing promises, they enjoy temporary popularity. However, God's judgment on false prophets is severe (Dt. 13:1-18).

John the apostle warned, "Do not believe every spirit, but test the spirits to see whether they are from God, for many false prophets have gone out into the world" (1 John 4:1). We must test all religious statements by the Bible.

The apostle Paul ranks the gift of prophecy among the most important gifts in the church. He urged his converts not to "quench the Holy Spirit," not to "despise prophecy," always to "test the messages of the prophets," and to "hold fast to the prophetic word by abstaining from every form of evil" (1 Thess. 5:19-22).

Sometimes, the gift of prophecy leads one to correct the church to bring it back to its proper nature and mission. Primarily, though, prophecy declares the good news of God's word to today's world.

2. Teaching

Understanding God's truth and communicating it clearly so others will grasp its relevance and importance for their lives (Romans 12:7; Eph. 4:11).

The New Testament word *didaskalia* means "teaching," "instruction," "that which is taught," or "doctrine." The noun *didaskalos* means "instructor" or "teacher"—"one who teaches the truths of God and the duties of people." The gift of teaching is a God-given ability to explain and apply the truths that God has revealed in scripture. This spiritual gift enables one to communicate more than factual information. God equips teachers to grasp and effectively to share the essence and heart of a Christian doctrine or biblical theme.

We need reliable teachers of God's truth because transmitters of Satan's lies try to deceive us with false teachings. Jesus said, "Whoever relaxes one of the least of these commandments and teaches others to do the same will be called least in the kingdom of heaven, but whoever does them and teaches them will be called great in the kingdom of heaven"(Matt 5:19).

A highly respected church historian wrote, "[The] heavenly body of apostolic truth is confronted with the ghost of heresy; as were the divine miracles of Moses with the satanic juggleries of the Egyptians....The more mightily the spirit of truth rises, the more active becomes the spirit of falsehood. Where God builds a church the devil builds a chapel close by."

Peter warned us about this. "False prophets also arose among the people, just as there will be false teachers among you, who will secretly  bring in destructive heresies [false teachings], even denying the Master who bought them, bringing upon themselves swift destruction" (2 Peter 2:1). False teachers are an outrage to God (1 Tim. 1:6-7).

The gift of teaching does not refer to sharing one's personal opinion or inner hunches. It involves  faithfulness to biblical truth. Jesus commissioned his disciples to teach everything *he* commanded them (Matt. 28:20). The apostle Paul's second letter to Timothy described those false teachers who do not base their teaching on God's word as "conceited, understanding nothing," and having "a morbid craving for controversy and for disputes about words" (2 Tim. 6:3-4)

When people become disciples of Jesus Christ they need instruction from Spirit-gifted teachers. The gift of teaching  is the God-given ability to understand and pass on God's word to others to affect their thinking, conduct, and world view. The outcome of the gift of teaching is to lead Christians to maturity, holiness, and good works. Because the authentic gift of teaching remains important for the well-being of the church, the Bible warns, "Not many of you should become teachers...for you know that we who teach will be judged with greater strictness" (James 3:1). Christian teachers should never rely on their own powers. The ability to clarify and teach divine truth becomes possible only by the supernatural enabling of the Holy Spirit. Nonetheless, God expects teachers to study and organize for their ministries. An American proverb says, "To fail to prepare is to prepare to fail."

If prophets call us to action, teachers provide sound instruction to guide us along the way. If prophets *preach* the word of God, teachers *explain* the word of God.

The Holy Spirit gives those with this gift an interest in truth and a love for study, even if it's hard work. They avoid mere human traditions, and teach God's trustworthy message set forth in the Bible.

Regrettably, some who teach lack the spiritual gift of teaching. Samuel Butler complained that university teachers "are too busy educating the young men to be able to teach them anything." The Holy Spirit gives teachers the ability to communicate spiritual truth effectively. Such anointed teaching sinks into the minds and hearts of others, and God's truth enlightens their understanding and transforms their lives.

3. Serving

Supporting others through Spirit-inspired service that lifts their loads and frees them for wider ministries (Rom. 12:7).

The New Testament uses the word *diakonia* to speak of those who serve others lovingly, as under a divine command to do so.

Translators sometimes rephrase *diakonia* as "ministry," "serving others," "service," and "helping others." The gift of serving fills one with the wish and the ability to understand and to serve the day-to-day needs of those whom God calls to broader public ministries. Jesus said that he came to earth as "the one who serves" and he frees us for "greater works."

Deacons in the Book of Acts served the apostles so they could "devote themselves to prayer, and to the ministry of the word" (Acts 6:4). An unknown poet captured the spirit of Christians who have the gift of serving:

> No service in itself is small,
> None great though earth it fill;
> But that is small that seeks its own
> And great that seeks God's will.

The word *deacon* suggests an attitude of humility and cheerfulness in attending to the needs of others. Those who serve do more than talk about ministering to others—they *do* it. This spiritual gift enables one to act appropriately, at the right time, in the right way, with the right attitude.

At the end of his letters St. Paul mentions the names of those whose service helped him to have a wider ministry. For instance, he spoke of how much good Onesiphorus did him by serving him: "He often  refreshed me and was not ashamed of my chain; when he arrived in Rome, he eagerly searched for me and found me—may the Lord grant that he will find mercy from the Lord on that day! And you know very well how much service [*diakonia*] he rendered" (2 Tim. 1:16-18). Paul prayed that his own service [*diakonia*] would "be acceptable to the saints" (Rom. 15:31).

Those who exercise this spiritual gift sometimes commit themselves to a long term of ministry to the people, organizations, and causes they serve. Christians with this gift do not use their service to promote themselves or gain recognition. They meet the needs of others without calling attention to their own ministries of serving. They receive fulfillment and joy in their helpful work and they find satisfaction in the words of Jesus who said, "The greatest among you will be your servant" (Matt. 23:11). The rewards of servers will be great. The Lord promised that when he returns he will invite those who served to sit at a table and he will put on an apron and serve *them*" (Luke 12:37).

4. Exhortation or Encouragement

Comforting and encouraging others, using the ministries of sympathetic understanding and scriptural counsel to cause right attitudes and actions (Rom. 12:8).

Translators of the New Testament noun *parakalon* translate it "exhort," "encourage," "urge," or "comfort." This word is the same word Jesus used to describe the Holy Spirit: "I will ask the Father, and he will give you another Advocate [*paraklatos*], to be with you forever" (John 14:16, 25).

This word includes the ideas of "encouragement," "comfort," "admonishment," "advocacy," "help," and "entreaty." This spiritual gift equips one to come alongside (*para*) others to encourage them and call (*kaleo*) out their potential. Paul wrote, "Encourage [*paraklesis*] one another and build up each other" (1 Thess. 5:11).

Biblical exhortation does not mean to berate people about their flaws and  failures. Rather, encouragers help others move ahead by guiding and lifting them up. Love, sympathy, and understanding provide exhorters with the power to inspire others to believe in the good future that God plans for them. Exhortation may sometimes call attention to another's need to change a flawed habit—while always trying to encourage and lift the person onto higher ground.

The Prophet Jeremiah spoke of encouragers who ministered "grace in the wilderness" (Jer. 31:2). The New Testament calls Barnabas a "son of encouragement," and he was an example of the spiritual gift of exhortation. He came to St. Paul's side and cheered him, even when the Jerusalem disciples shunned the great apostle. Barnabas also encouraged John Mark after he deserted the team during its first missionary trip. The gift of exhortation enables one to smile with both face and heart, while bringing out the best in others.

Timothy also was an encourager. St. Paul wrote him, "I solemnly urge you: proclaim the message; be persistent whether the time is favorable or unfavorable; convince, rebuke, and encourage, with the utmost patience" (2 Tim. 4:1-2).

Christian encouragers speak forthrightly, but kindly and hopefully. Their engaging ministry of exhortation hits the mark effectively, and they help others raise their sights, purify their aims, and deepen their commitments.

5. Giving

Supplying generous material or financial means to help others and to advance God's work in people's lives and in the church's ministries (Rom. 12:8).

The New Testament word *metadidous* means "one who gives, grants, or shares." This word comes from a verb *(didomi)* which can mean bearing fruit, coming from a seed. Different versions of the New Testament translate the word as "he who contributes," "he who gives to charity," "he who gives freely," and "almsgiving." The practical needs of others call for the proper distribution of material goods.

The spiritual gift of giving inspires and enables a ministry of wise sharing. Christians with the gift of giving contribute generously from hearts filled with love and liberality. God's givers do not share to gain God's favor, bribe him, or gain human applause. They give out of their grateful response to all he has done in their lives. They are wise investors in eternity.

Those with the gift of giving do not give at random, but with insight and good judgment. Unwise giving could bring more harm than blessing. Liberal and cheerful givers pray for God's wisdom to enable them to share wisely, selflessly, and cheerfully. An anonymous poet penned these encouraging words:

> Give strength, give thought,
>   give deeds, give wealth;
> Give love, give tears, and give
>   thyself.
> Give, give, be always giving,
> Who gives not is not living;
> The more your give, the more
>   you live.

A wisely chosen gift at the right time becomes a double blessing to others.

Givers find that when they give according to their ability, God expands their means in line with their giving. One need not be wealthy to have the gift of giving. Some give joyfully, even though they have very limited means. Sometimes God values the "widow's mite" more than enormous sums given in the wrong spirit or to the wrong cause (Mark 12:42-44). The more generous we become, the more God enables us to gain so we can give still more.

In his famous book *The Pilgrim's Progress*, John Bunyan wrote,

> A man there was,
> though some did count him mad,
> The more he cast away
> the more he had.

Generous people know the truth of St. Paul's quotation from Jesus that one finds blessing more in giving than in receiving (Acts 20:35).

6. Giving Aid

Providing leadership to coordinate the materials and abilities of others to meet the practical needs of people and organizations (Rom. 12:8).

The New Testament word *proistamenos* means to "rule over," "preside," "lead," "superintend" or "stand before others as a guide." Bible translators transcribe this word as "leader," "protector," "champion," "patron," "one who governs," or "one who stands in front." Clearly, this gift refers to leadership. We can define this gift as leading others in providing pactical aid and support.

It is true that no Christian is "above" another, and all Christians have full access to the grace of

God. Still, God assigns positions of authority to some. The New Testament teaches that we should properly respect God's appointed leaders (Phil. 2:29). The Bible speaks of those who "rule well" as "considered worthy of double honor," and we should value these leaders and heed their words (1 Tim. 5:17). St. Paul wrote, "Respect those who labor among you, and have charge of you in the Lord...esteem them highly in love because of their work" (1 Thess. 5:12-13).

Henry Ford once cleverly remarked, "The question, 'Who should lead?' is like asking, 'Who should sing tenor in the quartet?' Obviously, the man who can sing tenor."

Spirit-gifted leaders sometimes make mistakes, as we all do. True leaders humbly admit their mistakes and work to correct them and repair the damage. Despite human flaws, our leaders' spiritual gifts can lift them above the limits of their natural abilities. Their task of leadership calls them to guide others in practical ministries with the spirit of wisdom, enthusiasm, and effective administration. This gift has less to do with position or office than with Spirit-anointed ability and personal integrity. Good leaders remain indispensable in the Christian community.

7. Compassion

Sensing needs in others, feeling sympathy, and cheerfully showing mercy and giving comfort (Rom. 12:8).

The Greek verb *eleeo* means to "have mercy on," "to comfort," "to feel sympathy with," or "to bring help." God is "rich in mercy" because of his "great love with which he loved us" (Eph. 2:4). In a court of law a person on trial seeks *eleos* from a judge, in hope of "mercy," kindness," and "goodwill." The spiritual gift of compassion enables one to sense others' hurts, empathize with them, and help carry their load. This quality is not the same as pity; it is heartfelt compassion for another person in physical or emotional pain. This spiritual gift includes both compassion and mercy. Those who have this gift minister with joy. St. Paul wrote, "He who does acts of mercy, with cheerfulness" (Rom. 12:8).

God wants us all to show compassion for others (Matt. 9:13), and this spiritual gift fills one with an extraordinary feeling for hurting people. The gift of compassion enables one to empathize with others' hurts and to minister mercy that heals, sets free, and makes new. This spiritual gift gives heaven-sent understanding that makes possible the healing of those with spiritual, emotional, and physical pain.

Handicapped and weakened people especially benefit from Christians who have the gift of compassion. Those who labor in hospitals, nursing homes, orphanages, and drug-treatment centers need this gift of the Holy Spirit. These kindhearted caregivers bring mercy, understanding, and sympathy to those who lack the ability to repay them.

They pray in the spirit of the following gospel song:

> Oh, to be like Thee,
> Full of compassion,
> Loving, forgiving, tender and kind,
> Helping the helpless,
> Cheering the fainting,
> Seeking the wand'ring
> Sinner to find.
>
> Oh, to be like Thee!
> Oh, to be like Thee,
> Blessed Redeemer,
> Pure as Thou art;
> Come in Thy sweetness,
> Come in Thy fullness;
> Stamp Thine own image
> Deep on my heart.

Often, people need more than medical or financial relief. Many long for the healing presence of someone who can sense their pain and lift their spirits. Compassion helps relieve their mental and emotional stress.  Those with this spiritual gift show mercy in ways that skillfully mediate God's compassion for hurting people.

King David declared in the Psalms, "The mercy of the Lord is from everlasting to everlasting upon them that fear him, and his righteousness unto children's children" (Psa. 103:17).

Throughout the Bible, mercy and compassion mark those who love God. Sadly, though, Christ's followers sometimes lack compassion. In her 1859 novel *Adam Bede* George Eliot remarked bitterly, "We hand folks over to God's mercy, and show none ourselves." Genuine compassion comes from God, who alone is the source of all mercy. The nineteenth-century author E. H. Chapin wrote, "Mercy among the virtues is like the moon among the stars—not so sparkling as many, but dispensing a calm radiance that hallows the whole." In an age of dry eyes, hot heads, lukewarm hearts, and cold feet, the world needs the mercy ministries of compassionate Christians.

8. Healing

Praying prayers of faith that bring God's healing to sick, frail, or disordered bodies, souls, and relationships (1 Cor. 12:9, 28, 30).

All healing has its source in God. Healers do not heal—God does. In the Old Testament God said, "I am the Lord your healer" (Ex.15:26). In listing the spiritual gifts, St. Paul uses the phrase as a double plural—"gifts of healings." This grammatical construction suggests that God heals many kinds of weaknesses, including physical, mental, spiritual, and relational ones. Jesus performed healing miracles in all these areas, as did his apostles.

Another area of healing deals with damage passed through one or more generations of families—such as alcoholism, gambling, drug addiction, and sexual confusion. The gift of healing does not enable one successfully to see the healing of all people, always, of every ill. God gives specific gifts of healings for particular times and needs. Often, gifts of healings combine with the gift of faith.

God uses several methods of physical healing for our bodies.

(1) Sometimes God heals instantly. Acts tells the story about friends who daily carried a man lame from birth to the temple in Jerusalem. Seeing him, Peter "took him by the right hand and raised him up; and immediately his feet and ankles became strong" (Acts 3:7). The healing was instant.

(2) God often heals over time. During serious flu outbreaks, some slowly recover and eventually regain full health. These healings are progressive.

(3) God often uses medical science to heal sick people. Doctors, nurses, and "miracle medicines" are blessings from God. Medicines and surgeries save countless lives.

(4) At other times, God does not restore our bodies to complete health, but gives us grace to endure the suffering and live a victorious life. In the summer of 1967, Joni Eareckson, a teenager, dived into the shallow water of Chesapeake Bay. Striking her head on a rock,

she severed her spinal cord and became a quadriplegic. Now in adult life, Joni's triumphant life proves that God's grace can lift us above physical handicaps. Nor did God heal the apostle Paul. Rather, God gave him grace to live victoriously with his physical affliction (2 Cor. 12:7-9).

(5) Finally, God will always heal us in the coming resurrection. The Book of Revelation promises resurrected bodies for God's people: "[God] will wipe every tear from their eyes; there shall be an end to death, and to mourning and crying and pain; for the old order has passed away!" (Rev. 21:4).

God prolonged his gifts of healings beyond the New Testament era, and he continues these gifts today. As with the other gifts of the Spirit, gifts of healings enable Christians to become God's channels, through which he ministers grace and blessing to hurting people. We must remember that our healer is God, not the person through which healing may come.

9. Working Miracles

Trusting God to work supernaturally in people and healing, freeing from evil spirits, and delivering from dangers (I Cor. 12:10, 28-29).

The Greek phrase *energemata dunameon* translates "one who works powers." These two Greek words produced our English words energy and dynamite. Translators restate this phrase "power for doing miracles," "mighty works," "miraculous powers," "working wonders," "the use of spiritual powers," and "the power of miracles."

We may define a miracle as a work that God alone can do. Miracles are supernatural works which natural agents and ordinary means cannot duplicate. Most versions of the Old Testament translate this word as "a wonder" or "a mighty work." New Testament scholars usually translate this word as "signs and wonders" (John 2:11).

The Book of Acts uses the word *dunameon* for the casting out of evil spirits and for physical healings.

Detecting the Treasure 41

This gift, however, involves much more than these two actions. The early Christians prayed, "Lord, look at their threats, and grant to your servants to speak your word with all boldness, while you stretch out your hand to heal, and signs and wonders are performed through the name of your holy servant Jesus" (Acts 4:29-30).

As is the case with every spiritual gift, this gift does not make a person superior to others. Writing about those who boast of their abilities, St. Paul said, "When they measure themselves by one another, and compare themselves with one another, they do not show good sense" (2 Cor. 10:12). The Book of Proverbs reminds us, "Pride goes before destruction, and a haughty spirit before a fall" (Prov. 16:18). The Holy Spirit gives the gifts of the Spirit as it pleases him, and we can take no credit for the gifts he supplies.

Although Jesus worked miracles, he refused to prove that he was sent from God by performing miracles for his skeptical critics (Matt. 12:38-42). He did not approve of those who demanded a supernatural sign before they would accept him as Lord. He declared, "A wicked and adulterous generation looks for a miraculous sign" (Matt. 16:4).

Jonathan Swift, the eighteenth-century Irish minister and author of *Gulliver's Travels*, spoke about those in his day who demanded miracles: "Religion seems to have grown faint with age," he said, "and requires miracles to nurse it." Nonetheless, God still works miracles as he chooses.

St. Luke reported that "God did extraordinary miracles through Paul" (Acts 19:11). He worked miracles of healing, cast out evil spirits, and performed wonders within nature. Paul wrote to the Galatian church, "that God gave them the Holy Spirit to work miracles in their midst" (Gal. 3:5).

The greatest of God's miracles are not physical, but spiritual. Most great men and women in the Bible performed no visible miracles at all. Jesus said of John the Baptizer, "Truly, I tell you, among those born of women no one has arisen greater than John the Baptist" (Matt. 11:11). Yet John's ministry saw no miracles (John 10:41). One may faithfully serve God for a lifetime without performing a scientific miracle.

Still, a number of Christians report clear accounts of God's miraculous powers at work today. Undeniably, God works more miracles in our world than we recognize. God prevents accidents, reverses sickness, stops the course of evil, and helps us overcome seemingly impossible obstacles. Undoubtedly, the greatest miracle of all is God's power to change human hearts and give new life in Jesus Christ. And all people can experience this work of God.

10. Tongues

Speaking in another earthly language or in an unknown language as a means of petition, praise, or thanksgiving (1 Cor. 12:10, 28).

Speaking in tongues enables one to speak in another language without having learned it. Usually, the gift of tongues voices a language the speaker and most hearers do not understand. An example of tongues-speaking in human languages appears in the Book of Acts, when others heard some of the Christians "speaking in the native language of each" (Acts 2:4-6). No interpretation was necessary, because the assembled people understood them (Acts 2:6-11). In our time, some missionaries report occasional instances when this occurs, even if rare.

An example of speaking in unknown tongues that could not be understood by the hearers appears in 1 Corinthians: "Those who speak in a tongue do not speak to other people but to God; for nobody understands them" (1 Cor. 14:2). When this practice occurs publicly, there must be an interpreter. Otherwise, St. Paul stated, "If the whole church comes together and all speak in tongues, and outsiders or unbelievers enter, will they not say that you are out of your mind?" (1 Cor. 14:23). So any public use of tongues needs an interpretation.

Besides the true gift of speaking in tongues, there are two kinds of tongues that are *not* gifts of the Spirit—*psychological* tongues and *demonic* tongues. An example of psychological tongues occurs when someone uses various techniques to "teach" others to speak in tongues. In some circles, teachers insist that all Christians can and should speak in tongues. Sometimes, group pressure causes a person to try in a sputtering way to "say something in tongues." People can fake this spiritual gift. This sort of speaking in tongues is not genuine, and it will fade away.

The second type of false tongues comes from demonic sources. For example, Pythia, an ancient priestess at Delphi in Greece, spoke in tongues. She inhaled volcanic fumes, chewed mind-altering laurel leaves, and fell into delirium and convulsions, which inspired her to speak rambling sounds. The pagan priests of Delphi interpreted these sounds as words from the god Apollo. This demonic form appears in certain sects of Hindu, Moslem, Voodoo, and Santeria practitioners.

We must reject tongues that are not valid, while recognizing valid tongues as authentic. St. Paul addressed tongues-speaking church members who uttered enthusiastic, but meaningless and senseless sounds. About this practice, 1 Corinthians 14 teaches eight principles.

1. Speaking publicly in "unknown" tongues is meaningless without an interpretation (1 Cor. 14:9).
2. When speaking in tongues the mind is not in control of what it says (1 Cor. 14:14).
3. Those who speak in tongues "build up" themselves, but not the congregation (1 Cor 14:4, 6, 9-11).
4. "Those who speak in tongues do not speak to the gathered assembly, but to God" (1 Cor. 14:2).
5. Speaking in tongues is not a sign for believers, but for unbelievers (1 Cor. 14:22).
6. There must be an interpretation if public utterances in tongues have meaning for other worshippers (1 Cor. 14:5, 28).
7. It is preferable to speak five words of prophecy than 10,000 words in tongues; therefore, the church should limit the use of tongues in public worship (1 Cor. 14:27-28).
8. Teachers act irresponsibly to insist that others must speak in tongues. No Christian has every spiritual gift (Rom. 12:6; 1 Cor. 12:29) and God gives out his gifts according to his sovereign will (1 Cor. 12:11).

Speaking in tongues can be a sign for some, but it is not *the* sign for all. Every Christian can know the fullness of the Holy Spirit without speaking in tongues. We can allow differences about this gift without breaking fellowship with other Christians who may disagree with us.

Christians who worship the same Lord are one in Jesus Christ, apart from whether they do, or do not, speak in tongues.

11. Interpretation of Tongues

Making clear to others the meaning or intent of what one says when speaking in an unknown tongue (1 Cor. 12:10, 30).

The gift of interpretation of tongues is a logical and necessary complement to speaking in tongues. The authoritative *Dictionary of Pentecostal and Charismatic Movements* defines the gift of interpretation of tongues as the gift "by which one so endowed makes clear to the congregation the unintelligible utterance of one who has spoken in tongues."

Scripture tells us that if one speaks publicly in a tongue, there must be an interpretation of the prayer request, praise, or thanksgiving. This gift enables one to understand what is being said in tongues and explain what is otherwise nonsense. It is not an intellectual understanding of what is said or a word-for-word "translation" of the words spoken in an unknown tongue. Rather, it is a spiritual interpretation of the sense of what the speaker said.

Sometimes the one who speaks in tongues can interpret what he or she has spoken. Indeed, St. Paul advised, "One who speaks in a tongue should pray for the power to interpret" (1 Cor. 14:13). Usually, someone other than the one who speaks in tongues interprets the words to the congregation.

God does not give "messages" to the congregation in tongues. Scripture says that those who speak in tongues do so to God. Paul insisted, "Those who speak in a tongue do not speak to other people but to God" (1 Cor. 14:2). Therefore, the interpretation should address words to God—such as praise, prayer, petition, or thanksgiving.

12. Word of Wisdom

Receiving a Spirit-assisted illumination that enables one to understand and share the mind of the Holy Spirit in a specific circumstance (1 Cor. 12:8)

The Bible distinguishes God's wisdom from human wisdom. Without God's help all human wisdom proves inadequate. James the apostle declared that much human wisdom is "earthly, natural, and demonic" (James 3:15). He also stated that God will give true wisdom if we pray for it (James 1:5). The Greek phrase for the gift of the word of wisdom is *logos sophias*. *Logos* (word) can mean "teaching," "doctrine," "communication," or "message." *Sophia* (wisdom) can mean "understanding," "insight," "good sense," "judgment," "sanity," and "the ability to grasp the heart of a matter." Translators interpret this spiritual gift as "the ability to give wise advice," "the utterance of wisdom," "the gift of wise speech," "speaking with wisdom," and "speaking with wisdom according to the Spirit."

The spiritual gift of the word of wisdom does not primarily concern our natural mental powers. Rather, it refers to heaven-sent understanding. Compared to divine wisdom, human wisdom is "foolishness with God" (1 Cor. 1:20; 3:19). St. Paul defined God's wisdom as "not a wisdom of this age or of the rulers of this age, who are doomed to perish [but] God's wisdom, secret and hidden, which he decreed before the ages for our glory" (1 Cor. 2:6-7). The word of wisdom enables one to understand from God's perspective, and speak or write with keen perception and sound judgment.

Of course, learning and experience will bring a measure of wisdom. The spiritual gift of the word of wisdom, though, is a heightened wisdom that God gives through the Holy Spirit. This spiritual gift does not bring complete wisdom about everything. It is a *word* of wisdom inspired by the Holy Spirit that helps guide a decision. This gift gives special understanding that transcends mere human insight, and it sweeps away doubt and confusion.

A word of wisdom can silence wrong advice, expose false teaching, and prevent unwise decisions. Often, Christians express joy and agreement when one speaks such words of wisdom. Jesus promised the early apostles, "I will give you words and a wisdom that none of your opponents will be able to withstand or contradict" (Luke 21:15).

In Acts 4 the Sanhedrin summoned the apostles Peter and John to rebuke them for preaching the resurrection of Jesus. These apostles amazed and confounded the Jewish Council with the wisdom of their words. We read further that Stephen's opponents "could not withstand the wisdom and the Spirit with which he spoke" (Acts 6:10).

When a Christian group faces a difficult decision, the Holy Spirit often gives someone with this gift a word of wise insight that plainly becomes the right word at the right time. When human understanding falls short, we need such Spirit-inspired wisdom.

Often, a few words and a short sentence serve well. A word of wisdom relaxes the atmosphere and lights up the right course of action. The Holy Spirit continues today to reveal words of wisdom through his servants to enable them to communicate God's perspective.

We see this spiritual gift at work in Acts, Chapter 15. That chapter records the first conference of the Christian church. James, the leader of the conference, used the gift of a word of wisdom to counsel wisely about Jewish law and Christian freedom.

Today, the Christian community needs the counsel of heaven-inspired servants of God. Perhaps Jesus would say again, "He who has an ear, let him hear what the Spirit says to the churches" (Rev. 2:7).

13. Word of Knowledge

Knowing a fact or circumstance based on direct illumination by the Holy Spirit (1 Cor. 12:28).

The Greek word *ginosko* means "to understand," "to recognize," and "to know." We can translate the biblical phrase *logos gnoseos* (word of knowledge) "the utterance of knowledge by the Spirit," "putting the deepest knowledge into words," "speaking with knowledge," or "speaking instruction by the Spirit." The gift of the word of knowledge enables one to realize something with certainty because the Holy Spirit reveals it. Jesus had a word of knowledge when he told the Samaritan woman she had been married five times, and the man she lived with was not her husband (John 4:18).

God gave Peter a word of knowledge about Ananias: "Why has Satan filled your heart to lie to the Holy Spirit and to keep back part of the proceeds of the land?" (Acts 5:1-3).

By this gift the Holy Spirit imparts a certainty to our words and uses them to help us in doing ministry. For example, before one prays for someone's healing, God may give the praying person a precise word of knowledge about what God is doing.

Throughout history, some have claimed special knowledge that makes them superior to others. In the first centuries, false teachers, called Gnostics, pretended special knowledge, known to them alone.

They charged fees to share it. Christianity has no secrets, because Christ revealed the kingdom of God to all people.

The spiritual gift of the word of knowledge comes from the Holy Spirit. St. Paul tells us that only in Christ do we find "the treasures of wisdom and knowledge" (Col. 2:2-3). This gift does not make one superior to others. Rather the word of knowledge enables us to help and encourage others. The Holy Spirit gives words of knowledge to guide our prayers, decisions, and service.

14. Faith

The Spirit-given ability to believe that because God is able to do wonderful works, we can trust him to bring them to pass in response to prayer and faith (1 Cor. 12:9).

The New Testament word *pistis* (faith) has several meanings. The context decides which one applies. Faith can mean "a conviction of the truth of something," "trust," "trustworthiness," "fidelity," "what one believes," or "assurance that God is at work."

In the New Testament, faith can also mean a spiritual fruit (Gal. 5:22). Later, we will see the difference between spiritual fruit and spiritual gifts. We are concerned here with faith as a spiritual gift. The gift of faith means mountain-moving belief that God is working in our world (Matt. 17:20).

The gift of faith brings a firm assurance that God enters our daily lives and he can work wonders. This faith brings extraordinary trust in God's divine action, even if plain facts seem to contradict it. Moses, for example, believed against all odds that God would miraculously deliver the Hebrew people from bondage. "By faith he left Egypt, unafraid of the king's anger; for he persevered as though he saw him who is invisible" (Heb. 11:27). Joshua and Caleb trusted God to lead the Israelites into the Promised Land. We have no power or authority to demand that God will intervene in certain ways. Yet, when God inspires faith, we have a sure conviction that God will bring to pass his remarkable work.

New Testament dictionaries define this meaning of faith as "a firm and welcome conviction." Often, the confidence that God will work wonderfully comes when others doubt that any solution is possible. Many Israelites doubted God's ability to give them victory over powerful enemies. Joshua and

Caleb, however, believed God's promise, and God rewarded their faith.

Most Christian institutions—such as missionary societies, schools, hospitals, campus ministries, orphanages, and service organizations—owe their beginnings to God's champions of faith.

Faith rarely brings instant answers. Usually, faith includes waiting, patience, and prayer. Today's hurried generation has developed an itch for instant results. In the Bible and throughout history, though, faith almost always has needed to deal with delay. In waiting, our main business is prayerfully to trust and obey God.

A certain species of bamboo, when planted, shows no signs of sprouting for a long time. For three years, the underground root must receive water and fertilizer—with no hint that the bamboo is alive. During the passing seasons, the plant does not sprout. But after a four-year wait the bamboo bursts from the soil and grows to a height of thirty or forty feet in a single season!

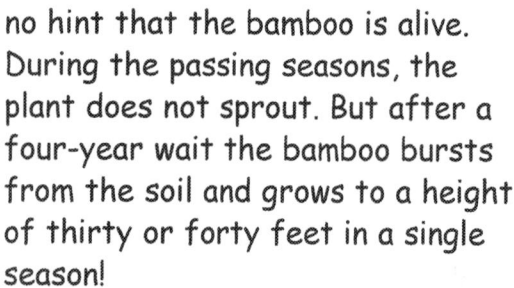

In a similar way, God works in our lives during our long waiting periods. Those with the gift of faith continue to trust, even when they see no immediate evidence of change. God works while we believe without seeing. Faith trusts that God will move in his own time and reward Spirit-inspired trust.

The gift of faith brings unshakable belief that God answers the prayers he inspires to release his blessings into our lives. The gift of faith encourages those of lesser faith and helps settle them in their walk with God. St. Augustine (354-430) wrote, "Faith is to believe what we do not see; and the reward of this faith is to see what we believe." Faith propels vision that paints a mental picture of what should be and will be.

15. Discernment of Spirits

Sensing whether a teaching or proposed action comes from a divine source, a human source, or an evil source (1 Cor. 12:10).

The full biblical name for the gift of discernment is "distinguishing of spirits," or "discernment of spirits." The Book of Hebrews speaks of "those

whose faculties have been trained by practice to identify the spiritual source of words and deeds" (Heb. 5:14). One New Testament paraphrase translates this gift as "knowing whether evil spirits are speaking through those who claim to be giving God's messages—or whether it is the Spirit of God who is speaking" (1 Cor. 12:10, *The Living Bible*).

Other versions of the Bible translate this gift as "the ability to distinguish between spirits," "the ability to distinguish true spirits from false," "to discriminate in spiritual matters," "the gift of recognizing spirits," or "the ability to discern whether a message is from the Spirit of God or from another spirit."

The Apostle Peter had the gift of discerning spirits. He saw through Simon Magus's evil deception and exposed it as "satanic" (Acts 8:20). Paul discerned the evil intent of a false prophet, whom he called "a son of the devil" (Acts 13:10). The spiritual gift of discernment enables the church to sort out what comes from the Holy Spirit, human spirits, and evil spirits.

Jesus warned, "Beware of false prophets, who come to you in sheep's clothing but inwardly are ravenous wolves....Many false prophets will arise and lead many astray" (Matt. 5:15; 24:11). The apostle Paul clarified that "our struggle is not against enemies of blood and flesh, but against the  rulers, against the authorities, against the cosmic powers of this present darkness, against the spiritual forces of evil in the heavenly places" (Eph. 6:12). How can we know right from wrong? Spiritual discernment makes it possible to discriminate in such important matters.

Spacecrafts dare not change their vectors by a single degree. It might seem at first that a small deviation does not matter. However, the slightest error in the beginning will eventually take the spacecraft thousands of miles from its intended destination. Seemingly small errors may seem to be of no consequence at first, but they can lead us far from God's will and favor. Because false teachers can cleverly misinterpret the Bible, the gift of discernment helps keep the Christian community in God's truth and God's will.

Paul reminded us that some teachers are "false

apostles, deceitful workers, disguising themselves as apostles of Christ." He added, "And no wonder! Even Satan disguises himself as an angel of light. So it is not strange if his ministers also disguise themselves as ministers of righteousness" (2 Cor. 11:13-15). The Christian community needs always to "weigh what is said" (1 Cor. 14:29). St. Paul warned, "Some will renounce the faith by paying attention to deceitful spirits and teachings of demons, through the hypocrisy of liars whose consciences are seared with a hot iron" (1 Tim. 4:1-2).

Billy Graham once wrote, "I am convinced that hundreds of religious leaders throughout the world are servants not of God, but of the Antichrist. They are wolves in sheep's clothing; they are tares instead of wheat." It's been that way for centuries.

Looking to the future, St. John wrote, "Beloved, do not believe every spirit, but test the spirits to see whether they are from God, for many false prophets have gone out into the world" (1 John 4:1). St. Paul advised, "Examine everything carefully; hold fast to that which is good" (1 Thess. 5:21). We can thank God for his sensitive servants with the gift of discerning spirits.

16. Apostleship

Transplanting the Gospel to a new environment to begin a new Christian community among unreached people (1 Cor. 12:28; Eph. 4:11).

The Greek word *apostolos* and its Latin equivalent *missio* mean "one sent as a delegate," or "an emissary sent with a message." Apostles are Spirit-sent ambassadors who represent the Christian community in new places.

The gift of apostleship gives one the outlook and ability to take God's good news to those uninformed about the Christian message, and set up a new church. Therefore, all apostles are missionaries of some kind, but not necessarily foreign missionaries.

For example, beginning a church among an inner city gang calls for the gift of apostleship. Apostles must reach across cultural obstacles and sometimes language barriers in their missionary work among those who do not know or understand the Gospel of Christ. Ordinarily, those with the gift of apostleship also have the gifts of prophecy, teaching, and working miracles.

Many apostles appear in the New Testament besides the twelve disciples of Jesus. Paul (Rom. 1:1), James (Gal. 1:19), Barnabas (Acts 14:14), Andronicus (Rom. 16:7), Junias who was probably a female apostle (Rom. 16:7), Silvanus (1 Thess. 1:1; 2:7), and Timothy (1 Thess.1:1; 2:7) also did apostolic work. The apostle James "the Just" (the brother of Jesus), who was not one of the original twelve apostles, presided as an apostle over the first general conference of Christians in the Book of Acts (Acts 15:19-23).

Paul tells us, "Christ gave some, apostles; and some, prophets; and some, evangelists; and some, pastors and teachers; for the perfecting of the saints, for the work of the ministry, for the edifying [encouraging] of the body of Christ: till we all come in the unity of the faith, and of the knowledge of the Son of God, unto a perfect man, unto the measure of the stature of the fullness of Christ" (Eph. 4:11).

Who can doubt that Hudson Taylor's work in China, David Livingstone's work in Africa, E. Stanley Jones's work in India, and Bruce Olson's work in South America qualify as apostolic? They planted Christianity where it previously had no presence, and they left enduring spiritual triumphs. The church continues to need this gift of the Spirit until Christ comes again to sum up earthly history.

17. Helps

Unselfishly serving the needy through ministries of practical service (1 Cor. 12:28).

The Greek noun *antilapsis* means "helping" or "supporting." In 1 Corinthians the word especially refers to helping the powerless and needy. Different versions of the Bible speak of this gift of the Holy Spirit as "those who help others," "helpers" and "the ability to help others."

The word appears, for example, in 1 Thessalonians 5:14: "Now we exhort you, brethren...support [help] the weak, be patient toward all." The word appears in Acts, where the apostle Paul taught the Ephesian elders, "We must help the weak, remembering the words of the Lord Jesus, for he himself said, 'It is more blessed to give than to receive'" (Acts 20:35).

The gift of helps mainly concerns relieving the practical needs of poor, weak, and suffering people. In the Book of Acts we read about a woman named Dorcas "who was always doing good and helping the poor" (Acts 9:36, *The Living Bible*). Those who help see ways to aid those who carry heavy loads, and they find joy in reaching out to needy people with practical aid. They hold to the saying, "When a person is crushed by the world, an ounce of help is better than a pound of preaching."

Those with the gift of helps may not necessarily continue serving the same people or organizations for long periods of time. Yet, regardless of their circumstances they give themselves to helping needy people. They heed Jesus' teaching, "When you give alms, do not let your left hand know what your right hand is doing, so that your alms may be done in secret; and your Father who sees in secret will reward you" (Matt. 6:3-4).

Sometimes the best service comes from unrecognized hands, whose work on earth never receives notice or praise. In eternity these people of good works will receive their reward, for Jesus said, "Whoever gives you a cup of water to drink because you bear the name of Christ will by no means lose the reward" (Mark 9:40).

18. Administration

Setting goals, planning, and leading others to work harmoniously toward a common goal in the work of God (1 Cor. 12:28).

The original Greek noun *kubernatas* means ""steersman," "helmsman," or "governor." The verb form of the word means "to pilot" or "to direct." Biblical scholars translate the word *kubernasis* as "governments," "one who gets others to work together," "administrator," "the power to guide others," "those who direct," "wielders of spiritual power," "organizers," "rulers," and "good leaders." Some people refer to this gift as "leadership." Leadership, however, lies at the heart of this gift.

All groups of people need management and accountability. God has given the church gifted leaders who have the gift of administration. The Holy Spirit enables those with this gift to recognize possibilities in people and organizations and lead them in effective ways. This gift shows itself in good judgment, sound advice, wise organizational skills, and the ability to lead people. Like pilots of ships, they steer the organization through challenging seas to the desired destination.

While effective administrators listen to the opinions of others, they sometimes have to do what is right rather than what is popular or what conforms to the opinions of the majority.

In 1941 Winston Churchill humorously said to England's House of Commons, "I see it said that leaders should keep their ears to the ground. All I can say is that the British nation will find it very hard to look up to the leaders who are detected in that somewhat ungainly posture."

The more leadership responsibility one has, the more one must pray, keep close to biblical principles, and obey God's guidance. Often leaders must summon the courage to follow God rather than yield to the noisy demands of unwise or emotionally excited people.

Of course, the group must hold the leader accountable and require him/her to stick soundly to the principles taught in scripture. Bad leaders can take over only if their followers allow it. The American author Bayard Taylor (1825-78) wrote a perceptive piece on leadership titled "Self-Mastery." In that composition he said,

> He who would lead must first himself be led;
>
> Who would be loved be capable to love
>
> Beyond the utmost he receives, who claims
>
> The rod of power must first have bowed
>
> And being honored, honor what's above:
>
> This know the men who leave the world their names.

The New Testament commands leaders to hold to the highest ethical standards and show spotless moral conduct.

Titus in the New Testament had this spiritual gift. St. Paul left him in Crete to "straighten out what was left unfinished and appoint elders in every town" (Tit. 1:5). The gift of administration enables leaders to serve effectively in different administrative positions—including churches, schools, hospitals, mission agencies, and other Christian organizations. Factory workers, students, coaches, homemakers, and business and professional people also may have this gift. Today's church needs such God-anointed leaders.

19. Evangelism

A special ability to understand the grave condition of unsaved people and lead them to commit their lives to Jesus Christ as their savior (Eph. 4:11).

The Greek word *euangelistas* means "a messenger of good news," "a bringer of good tidings," or "an evangelist." The gift of evangelism is the Spirit-given ability to share the Christian gospel with clarity, skill, and conviction. This gift equips Christians to win others to Christ by public speaking, writing, or personal conversation. The content of an evangelist's message is the *euangelion*, which means "gospel," or "good news."

The gift of evangelism enables some Christians to be very successful in personal evangelism, but not in evangelistic preaching. Others win many to Christ through evangelistic preaching, but not through personal evangelism. Still others excel in both forms of evangelism. God calls some Christians to evangelistic writing. And awesome is the power of an upright and holy life.

The success of evangelism does not depend on our efforts, but on God's working through the Holy Spirit. Using gimmicks, unbiblical promises, or manipulative techniques is unnecessary and misguided. All genuine conversions to Christ come from the work of God. John's Gospel tells us, "To all who received him [Christ], who believed in his name, he gave power to become children of God, who were born, not of blood, or of the will of the flesh or of the will of man, but of God" (John 1:13). This spiritual gift, like all the others, is not a mere human ability, but a divine enabling.

Those with this spiritual gift cannot escape from the thought of lost people who lurch toward God's final judgment without knowing Jesus Christ as savior. The gift of evangelism gives one an overriding concern to bring the lost to accept Jesus Christ as Savior and Lord. Soul winners do not call attention to themselves or to their church so much as they exalt Jesus Christ, and point to his sacrificial death for sinners.

People can become Christians only if others introduce them to Jesus

Christ. Prophets point to the way; teachers explain the way; shepherds lead others along the way; and evangelists focus on bringing people into the way.

20. Shepherding

Leading and serving others through the pastoral ministries of teaching, guiding, and nurturing to bring them to Christian maturity and Christ-likeness (Eph. 4:11).

The original Greek word *poimān* means "shepherd." The New Testament uses this word in three ways.

(1) The ordinary use of the word refers to those who tend flocks. For instance, one of the sons of Adam and Eve was Abel, who was a shepherd (Gen. 4:2). In the New Testament we read, "There were shepherds living in the fields, keeping watch over their flock by night" (Luke 2:8).

(2) As well as the normal use of the word, the New Testament uses "shepherd" to refer to Christ. Peter referred to him as "the shepherd and guardian" of our souls (1 Peter 2:25). The writer of Hebrews speaks of Jesus as a shepherd in an often-quoted blessing: "Now the God of peace, who brought again from the dead the great shepherd of the sheep with the blood of an eternal covenant, even our Lord Jesus, make you perfect in every good thing to do his will, working in us that which is well-pleasing in his sight, through Jesus Christ; to whom be the glory for ever and ever" (Heb. 13:20-21).

(3) A third New Testament use of the term "shepherd" is for a pastor who is the leader of a Christian community. St. Paul speaks of the pastor as one who "shepherds" a flock. All genuine pastors are assistants to "the great Shepherd of the sheep," Jesus Christ (Acts 20:28). And true pastors are willing to lay down their lives for the sheep (John 10:11).

One of the chief roles of a shepherd is to teach. In Ephesians 4:11 St. Paul closely links pastoring and teaching. One may have the gift of teaching without the gift of shepherding. Pastors, however, must have the gift of teaching. They can teach without pastoring a church, but they cannot pastor without teaching. Any true pastor must teach others the word of God. Indeed, teaching and preaching God's word is the pastor's principle duty. The New Testament holds pastors responsibleto teach others to follow the Great Shepherd.

The New Testament uses the terms "elder" and "overseer" to describe pastors. They are responsible to protect, feed, and guide the flock God entrusts to them. These important tasks call for the power of the Holy Spirit flowing through the gift of shepherding, or pastoring.

One does not need to be ordained as a minister or hold a pastoral office to exercise the gift of shepherding. Many church people do the work of a pastor. A teenager, for example, can watch over classmates and help guide them. A factory worker can shepherd a cluster of friends and co-workers. A homemaker can shepherd younger women by teaching them, building them up, and guiding them. Youth directors, Sunday school teachers, and office workers can and do serve as pastors among those they serve. Pastors can use the help of church members who also have the gift of shepherding. Wise is the pastor who recognizes and uses such gifted church members.

The New Testament insists that those with the gift of shepherding lead godly lives that are pure and mature. They must "set an example...in speech, in life, in love, in faith and in purity" (1 Tim. 4:12). St. Paul wrote Titus, "Since an overseer is trusted with doing God's work, he must be blameless—not overbearing, not quick-tempered, not given to drunkenness, not violent, not pursuing dishonest gain." God calls shepherds to "love what is good and be self-controlled, upright, holy, and disciplined" (Tit. 1:6-9).

Final Thoughts

All these New Testament gifts of the Spirit continue today. As God gives them to Christians, the body of Christ will "come to unity in faith and knowledge of God's Son that they will become mature in the Lord, and measure up to the full and complete standard of Christ" (Eph. 4:13, NLT). God's kingdom will become richer and fuller as you contribute your personal ministries through the spiritual gifts that God graciously gives you. Knowing and using your *charismata* forms the foundation for a productive life that brings rewards now and forever.

People Watchers
(A Group Activity)

Some people complain that hidden security cameras invade our privacy. Whether we have too many security cameras, we're all incurable people watchers. Let's face it—babies watch their mothers and fathers; students study their teachers (sometimes more than their lessons); boys watch girls; girls watch boys; mall sitters inspect those who parade past them; people watch people who watch people. We're incurable people watchers.

And in one way or another we influence and we are swayed by others—even if we don't speak a word. Benjamin Franklin said, "None preaches better than the ant, and she says nothing."

Without doubt, we evaluate others less by what they claim to be than by what we see them do. Bad examples and good examples speak volumes and influence people much more than we can imagine. Much of the time we are not fully aware of the examples we set. Yet, as certain as the sun rises and as surely as security cameras scan our faces, others see our influence. If you are alert, you can spot in dedicated Christians clear signs that Christ lives in them and works through them.

This chapter described each of the New Testament gifts of the Holy Spirit. Break into groups and keep this book with you, which lists the gifts on the back cover. Probably, as you read the preceding pages you thought of those who had certain spiritual gifts in their lives. Tell about someone you've known who displayed by their life one or more of the spiritual gifts discussed in this chapter.

> What spiritual gift did you see in him or her?
> How did it show itself?
> Did it have a moving effect on others?
> What specific result did you see in their ministry?
> Have your observations of others helped confirm the reality of some of the gifts described in this chapter?

Set the Example

"Don't let anyone look down on you because you are young, but set an example for the believers in speech, in life, in faith and in purity" (1 Tim 4:12)

"In everything set them an example by doing what is good" (Titus 2:7)

"By faith he [Abel] still speaks, even though he is dead
(Heb. 11:4)

4

Discerning the Distinctions

"Now, concerning spiritual gifts, brothers and sisters, I do not want you to be uninformed." So wrote the apostle Paul. Today, we face the same problems that challenged the first-century Christians. In our time as in St. Paul's, ignorance, confusion, and doubt still linger. We can compare these obstacles to a tangled ball of kite string that limits our ability to guide the kite into the wind. This chapter looks at three common tangles that sometimes slow us down.

1. Whether Spiritual Gifts Are the Same As the Fruit of the Spirit

Christians sometimes confuse spiritual *gifts* with spiritual *fruits*. These two works of God are distinct from each other. In his letter to the Christians at Galatia, St. Paul lists the fruit of the Spirit as love, joy, peace, patience, kindness, generosity, faithfulness, gentleness, and self-control (Gal. 5:22-23).

Spiritual fruits are *moral virtues* that define holiness, maturity, and Christ-likeness. Evidence of these qualities in our lives points to our growing maturity as disciples of the living Lord.

By contrast, spiritual gifts are not moral virtues. Rather, they are God's offer of spiritual power and supernatural ability. If spiritual fruit concerns *character*, spiritual gifts relate to *service*. If spiritual fruit concerns who we *are*, spiritual gifts concern what we *do*. Spiritual gifts are the tools and abilities God gives us to minister and serve. For example, the gift of teaching is not a moral virtue. It is an anointing from God that enables us to teach

God's truth in ways not possible with natural talent alone.

We can summarize the differences between spiritual gifts and spiritual fruit in the following chart.

Spiritual Fruit	Spiritual Gifts
God intends all the fruit of the Spirit for all Christians.	God intends different gifts for different Christians.
Spiritual fruit demonstrates character and holiness.	Spiritual gifts enable ministry and empower service.
Christians can expect *all* the fruit of the Spirit.	Christians can expect some of the gifts of the Spirit.
All spiritual fruit is essential.	Some gifts are more essential than others.
Spiritual fruit cannot be abused; it leads to unity.	Spiritual gifts can be abused and lead to strife and division.

2. Whether Spiritual Gifts Are the Same as Human Talents or Developed Skills

Some Christians confuse the gifts of the Holy Spirit with our natural or learned abilities. Human talents and expertise are admirable qualities, of course. Yet, these innate abilities can work without our relying on the Holy Spirit. Talented people can accomplish impressive feats. From time to time, such people can win a following, invent useful tools, paint beautiful portraits, write touching songs, attract votes, or design impressive buildings.

Sometimes, though, human accomplishments can do more harm than good. Those who rely on their natural abilities cannot achieve their highest potential or enjoy God's full blessings. Human endeavors, as sparkling and impressive as they might be, are by themselves not sufficient to build God's kingdom or win his approval.

At least six differences summarize the distinctions between human talents and spiritual gifts.

Human Talents and Abilities	Gifts of the Holy Spirit
We inherit human talents at birth.	We receive spiritual gifts at the new birth.
Human talents are natural, and they come through our parents and ancestors.	Spiritual gifts are supernatural, and they come from the Holy Spirit.
All people have talents and natural abilities.	Only Christians receive the gifts of the Spirit.
Human abilities can function apart from the Holy Spirit.	Gifts of the Spirit cannot flow freely without the Holy Spirit.
Talents glorify people.	Spiritual gifts glorify God.
Talents work on the natural level and bring temporal results.	Spiritual gifts work on a supernatural plane and bring eternal results.

A talented soprano with uncommon natural abilities may delight thousands of admiring listeners and win the respect of music critics. Yet such human talents are not spiritual gifts. To be sure, Christians should develop their natural talents. God can and does use them. Yet, without spiritual gifts we cannot minister well enough to do God's kingdom work. Suppose, for example, the talented soprano had the spiritual gift of evangelism. With her ministry of singing she might become an instrument for bringing many people to faith in Jesus Christ.

Sometimes a person with a natural talent may also have a spiritual gift in the same vein. For instance, a person with speaking skills might also have the gift of prophecy. In such cases, God intensifies a natural ability by raising it to the higher level of a spiritual gift.

At the same time, the most unlikely person might receive a spiritual gift that we would not have expected. Moses was "slow of speech and slow of tongue." Yet God gifted him to lead the Hebrew people from Egyptian slavery to the Land of Promise, and deliver God's

Ten Commandments to the people.

Those who may lack impressive human abilities can carry out mighty deeds if God works through them by his Spirit. For example, a piano by itself cannot produce music. Melody comes only when the hands of an expert controls the instrument.

Jesus said, "I am the vine, you are the branches. Those who abide in me and I in them bear much fruit, because apart from me you can do nothing" (John 15:5). The prophet Zechariah declared God's eternal message, "This is the word of the Lord...Not by might, nor by power, but by my spirit, says the LORD of hosts" (Zech. 4:6).

Our talents and spiritual gifts come from God, and he uses both. Artistic, musical, surgical, mechanical, and intellectual abilities have their source in God the Creator. St. James reminds us, "Every good endowment and every perfect gift is from above, coming down from the Father" (James 1:17). Here, for "gift" James uses the word *dorama*, not *charismata*. *Dorama* means "beautiful gift," such as the sunshine, rain, and fruiting trees. For Christian work, the New Testament stresses the need for the *charismata*, meaning "spiritual gifts." These gifts come to us through the Holy Spirit, and they focus on the most important ministries of the church. We do well to give attention to them.

3. Whether Personality Traits, Special Graces, Church Offices, and Religious Ministries Are Gifts of the Holy Spirit

Some teachers confuse spiritual gifts with personality characteristics. One conference speaker stated, "I believe there are hundreds of spiritual gifts such as being friendly, keeping serious, having a sense of humor, playing tennis, shopping for bargains, and having the skill to decorate a room." The speaker went on to say that he had the spiritual gift of being an extrovert, his wife had the spiritual gift of being beautiful, and his daughter had the spiritual gift of wise shopping.

The qualities of "being friendly," "being serious" and "being thrifty" are not spiritual gifts. Also, whether we are introverts or extroverts does not determine our spiritual gifts. Some with the gift of evangelism radiate outgoing personalities; others with the same gift project quiet behavior traits. Some people with the gift of administration sparkle with humor.

Other people with quiet personalities are equally gifted and effective administrators. The spiritual gifts are the same, but our temperaments differ.

A well-meaning teacher wrote that spiritual gifts include "suffering," "voluntary poverty," "humor," "craftsmanship," "Spirit-music," "prayer," "singleness," "hospitality," and "battle." Another writer includes in his list of spiritual gifts such traits as "friendliness," "optimism," "cheerfulness," "persistence," "thriftiness," "generosity," "neatness of dress," and "selling skills." These attitudes, ministries, and characteristics do give evidence of God's help for daily living. They are not, however, New Testament gifts of the Holy Spirit. See page 25.

If spiritual gifts are not personality traits, neither are spiritual *graces*. Examples of spiritual graces include dying for one's faith in Christ (martyrdom), suffering severe persecution, living in extreme want, and a call to a single life. Christians whom God allows to die martyr's deaths, to suffer want, or to spend their lives in a monastery or nunnery receive the spiritual grace to do so. However, these graces are not spiritual gifts. Rather, they are God's special anointings for unusual circumstances.

> *Christ gave spiritual gifts to the church to prepare all God's people for the work of Christian service in order to build up the body of Christ. And so we shall all come together to oneness in our faith and in our knowledge of the Son of God; we shall become mature people, reaching to the very height of Christ's full stature.*
> —summarizing St. Paul

Sometimes, people muddle the distinction between spiritual gifts, official titles, and positions. One well-meaning teacher announced, "One of the important spiritual gifts is choir director." An office, such as a church leadership position, is not a spiritual gift. A position such as choir director, business manager, or bishop points to the ministry one has.

Of course, it may be that one who holds the office of pastor does not have the gift of shepherding. There are also people who hold teaching responsibilities, but lack the gift of teaching. It is true that some have the gift of teaching who do not hold a teaching office in the church. Or, one might have the gift of administration without holding an administrative position. The point here is that an office is not a gift, and a gift is not an office.

Finally, one's ministry, vocation, or calling is not a spiritual gift. A conference speaker said, "I think we need more people with the spiritual gifts of poet, mechanic, and computer expert." I read an author who claimed that spiritual gifts include "public speaking, ushering, coaching, cooking, and typing."

One woman told me her spiritual gift was "walking her dog." Another person said in all seriousness, "My spiritual gift is baking pies." A man in a large city said that his spiritual gift was being the mayor. Ministries, services, and careers are important, but they are not New Testament spiritual gifts.

One might have a calling of, say, coaching, cooking, teaching tennis, or grounds keeping. These ministries are necessary, but they are not spiritual gifts. The gifts of teaching and exhortation might flow through the ministry of coaching. The gifts of serving and giving aid might lead to a ministry of supervising church dinners. The gifts of evangelism, teaching, and the word of wisdom could accompany one's ministry of teaching tennis or grounds keeping. These callings are ministries, through which spiritual gifts find expression.

Summary

This chapter has focused on several necessary distinctions. We have seen that we should not confuse the gifts of the Spirit with the fruit of the Spirit. We also saw that spiritual gifts differ from natural talents, and we should distinguish spiritual gifts from personality traits, special graces, positions, and ministries. Of course it's more important to have a right heart than right opinions. Thankfully, though, we do not need to settle for one or the other. With God's help we can strive for both right living *and* right thinking.

Human Ability or Divine Power?
Discussion Suggestions

1. Discuss the relationship between what we are inwardly and what we do outwardly.
    - Constrast holiness of life with power to serve.
    - Can Christians misuse the divine power God gives them?
    - Have you seen any examples?
    - Talk about God's plan for us to have both a holy life and a powerful life. Why?

2. Discuss the contrast between human ability and divne enabling.
    - Why are godless people sometimes able to accomplish impressive achievements?
    - How can some of those who do not allow God in their lives have such brilliant minds?
    - Have someone read slowly and clearly 1 Cor. 1:22-31

> For Jews demand signs and Greeks desire wisdom, but we proclaim Christ crucified, a stumbling block to Jews and foolishness to Gentiles, but to those who are the called, both Jews and Greeks, Christ the power of God and the wisdom of God. For God's foolishness is wiser than human wisdom, and God's weakness is stronger than human strength. Consider your own call, brothers and sisters: not many of you were wise by human standards, not many were powerful, not many were of noble birth. But God chose what is foolish in the world to shame the wise; God chose what is weak in the world to shame the strong; God chose what is low and despised in the world, things that are not, to reduce to nothing things that are, so that no one might boast in the presence of God. He is the source of your life in Christ Jesus, who became for us wisdom from God, and righteousness and sanctification and redemption, in order that, as it is written, "Let the one who boasts, boast in the Lord."

—What was St. Paul saying about the relative merits of human ability and divine power?

—Discuss the difference between our ability and our availability.

SOME INTERESTING QUOTATIONS ABOUT CHARACTER...

"When one's character is right, one's appearance is a greater delight to others."
—Ovid, a Roman poet (43 B.C.-18 A.D.).

"Happiness is not the end of life: character is."
—Henry Ward Beecher, American clergyman (1813-1887), *Life Thoughts*, 1887.

"Nearly all men can stand adversity, but if you want to test a man's character, give him power."
—Abraham Lincoln (1809-1865), sixteenth president of the United States.

"Sow an act, and you reap a habit. Sow a habit, and you reap a character. Sow a character, and you reap a destiny."
—Charles Reade (1814-1884), British novelist, *Notes and Queries*.

"When you choose your friends, don't be short-changed by choosing personality over character."
—William Somerset Maugham (1874-1965) British author.

"Character is much easier kept than recovered."
—Thomas Paine, American patriot (1737-1809) *The American Crisis*, 1776.

5

Directing the Focus

The New Testament teaching about the gifts of the Holy Spirit includes seven principles. Sometimes the biblical writers teach them straightforwardly; at other times we see them indirectly. These principles do not come from just one or two verses of scripture. Rather, they appear in several New Testament books written by different authors. The *charismata* continue in our day, and the following biblical principles are still important.

1. All Christians Have Spiritual Gifts

First, God gives to every Christian one or more of the *charismata*. Writing to the Corinthian church about spiritual gifts, St. Paul affirmed that "To each is given the manifestation of the Spirit for the common good" (1 Cor. 12:7). Because God gives spiritual gifts to each of Christ's followers, there are no "ungifted" Christians.

God does not withhold certain gifts from people, based on their education, position, denomination, or intelligence. Whether male or female, lay or clergy, ordained or not ordained, all Christians receive God's gifts. No Christian has all the gifts of the spirit, but every Christian has at least one gift. God often endows people with several of these extraordinary abilities. Some Christians do not know their gifts. Other Christians who know their gifts neglect to use them. And a few misuse their gifts. Still, all Christians have spiritual gifts.

Paul reminded the church at Rome, "We have gifts that differ according to the grace given to us" (Rom. 12:6). Elsewhere, Paul taught, "There are varieties of gifts, but the same Spirit.... Indeed, the body does not consist of one member but of many" (1 Cor. 12:4, 8-10, 14). Because our gifts complement those of other Christians, each one is important for the community of Christian believers.

We cannot gain God's gifts by money or political means. God gives them to us because of his grace. Nowhere does the New Testament say that we can receive a spiritual gift by demanding it. The book of Acts tells the story of a pagan magician named Simon Magus who wanted to buy God's power. The apostle Peter rebuked him: "May your silver perish with you, because you thought you could obtain God's gift with money!" (Acts 8:20).

Certainly, you may *ask* for a specific gift. Scripture encourages us to aspire after spiritual gifts, but *asking* and *insisting* are not the same. Sometimes God does not give you the gift you think you want; sometimes he does. He may surprise you with gifts that you neither thought of nor asked for. We do know that God wants us to discover and use the spiritual gifts he plans for us. St. Paul encouraged the Corinthian church, "Eagerly desire spiritual gifts" (1 Cor. 14:1). As we remain fully open to the Giver of the gifts, we will discover the gifts of the Giver.

If all Christians discovered their spiritual gifts and used them faithfully, God would pour out wonderful blessings on his people. God's plan is to work through us to change the world. When individuals and congregations awaken to the power of the Holy Spirit, the Christian community begins to move more rapidly to fulfill its commission to make disciples of all nations. Every Christian is important to the proper functioning of the worldwide body of Christ. And each of us can make our maximum contribution by discovering and using our spiritual gifts.

2. God Gives Us Spiritual Gifts Apart from our Deserving Them

Second, we do not earn God's gifts. We have no more power to produce spiritual gifts than we have to save ourselves. St. James wrote, "Every desirable and beneficial gift comes out of heaven" (James 1:17). *Christ builds the church and it is he who equips us for every good work* (Matt. 16:18; 2 Tim 2:21). The Apostle Peter wrote, "God has given each of you a gift from his great variety of spiritual gifts. Use them well to serve one another" (1 Pet. 4:10).

Although God gives us spiritual gifts without our deserving or earning them, he expects us to be receptive and walk in His will. We must cooperate with God. He initiates, and he expects us to respond. St. Paul wrote, "Work out your own salvation...for it is God who works in you both to will and to do of his good pleasure" (Phil. 2:12-13). God does his part, and we must do ours.

God wants us to become part of his work on earth. George Eliot wrote a moving poem, "Stradivarius." [Stradivarius (1644-1737) made the world's finest violins].

> Your soul was lifted by the wings to-day
> Hearing the master of the violin:
> You praised him, praised the great Sabastian [Bach] too
> Who made that fine Chaconne;
> but did you think
> Of old Antonio Stradivari?—him
> Who a good centry and half ago
> Put his true work in that brown instrument
> And by the nice adjustment of its frame
> Gave it responsive life, continuous
> With the master's finger-tips and perfected
> Them by delicate rectitude of use...
> I say not God Himself can make man's best
> Without best men to help him...
> 'Tis God gives skill,
> But not without their hands: He could not make
> Antonio Stradivari's violins
> Without Antonio.

God knows where and how each Christian will fit into his master plan. As Christians humbly and gratefully surrender themselves to God's purpose, they find fulfillment, reach their potential, bring unity to the church, and gain eternal rewards. In the end, all our blessings come not from human merit or effort, but from the grace and goodness of God.

3. God Grants and Administers These Gifts According to His Perfect Will

Third, God distributes his gifts wisely. He assigns the *charismata* according to his will, not according to human wishes or demands. The Holy Spirit gives these gifts to "each one individually just as the

Spirit chooses" (1 Cor. 12:11). The Book of Hebrews states that God reveals himself by "signs and wonders and various miracles, and by gifts of the Holy Spirit, divided according to his will" (Heb. 2:4).

We are not wise enough or strong enough to distribute the gifts of the Spirit according to our own preferences. They are not the gifts of your church, denomination, parents, or leaders. They come to you as gifts of the Holy Spirit, and he alone shares them according to his wisdom and will. Jesus emphasized the self-governing work of the Holy Spirit: "The wind blows where it chooses, and you hear the sound of it, but you do not know where it comes from or where it goes. So it is with everyone who is born of the Spirit" (John 3:8).

We need humbly and gratefully to receive the gift or gifts that God assigns to us. It would be most ungrateful to say, "I don't like the spiritual gifts God gave me, and I want to trade them in for others. I want to be like so-and-so, to have his successes." God graces us with gifts perfectly suited to us. Our gifts may fit us to serve in a public and prominent way or in an anonymous and unrecognized way.

God uses us the way carpenters use tools. Saws cut boards; hammers fasten nails; sanders smooth surfaces; drills bore holes; rulers measure dimensions. Every member of the body is essential to the health and proper functioning of the body. 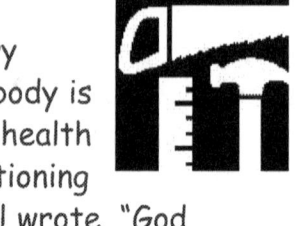 Paul wrote, "God arranged the members in the body, each one of them, as he chose. If all were a single member, where would the body be? As it is, there are many members, yet one body. The eye cannot say to the hand, 'I have no need of you,' nor again the head to the feet, 'I have no need of you.'" God the wise giver of gifts knows which ones suit us best. There is no place either for attitudes of pride or feelings of inferiority.

John Wesley prepared a Covenant Service for those who wanted to serve God with their whole heart, soul, mind, and strength. The words of this service contain the following prayer of commitment:

> Christ has many services to be done; some are easy, others are difficult; some bring honor, others bring reproach; some are suitable to our natural inclinations and temporal interests, others are contrary to both. In some we may please Christ and please

ourselves; in others we cannot please Christ except by denying ourselves. Yet the power to do all these things is assuredly given us in Christ, who strengthens us...

I am no longer my own, but thine. Put me to what thou wilt, rank me with whom thou wilt; put me to doing, put me to suffering; let me be employed for thee or laid aside for thee, exalted for thee or brought low for thee; let me have all things, let me have nothing; I freely and heartily yield all things to thy pleasure and disposal....And the covenant which I have made on earth let it be ratified in heaven. Amen.

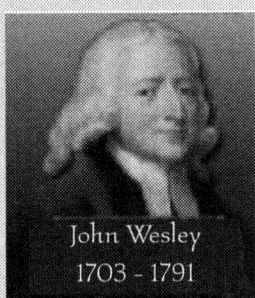

John Wesley
1703 - 1791

Scripture commands us joyfully to receive God's spiritual gifts, and to use them in ministry to others. God made each of us individually with a one-of-a-kind personality. That truth makes everyone unique, special, and valuable. God grants his grace-given *charismata* to us, and as we follow Christ, the Holy Spirit opens opportunities for us to use our gifts for God and others.

4. God Gives Gifts for Ministry and Service

Fourth, God does not give us gifts to satisfy our curiosity or build our egos. He gives us gifts to equip us for service and ministry. Scripture tells us that "to each is given the manifestation of the Spirit for the common good" (1 Cor. 12:7). There is an important link between our gifts and our service to others. The apostle Peter wrote, "Serve one another with whatever gift each of you has received" (1 Pet. 4:10).

St. Paul described the spirit of Christian service in his letter to the Philippian Church: "Do nothing from selfish ambition or conceit or from a cheap desire to boast, but be humbled toward one another, always considering others better than yourselves" (Phil. 2:3-4). Martin Luther wrote that Christians are the most free of all, yet at the same time "the most dutiful servants of all."

It is possible to mishandle or abuse the gifts God gives us. Misuse occurs when we use God's gifts to gain personal power, promote self-glory, or become greedy. These unworthy uses of spiritual gifts cause disunity among others. They lead to a blemished "ministry."

God intends that spiritual gifts

unite the body of Christ, never divide it. We should "make every effort to maintain the unity of the Spirit in the bond of peace" (Eph. 4:3). Jesus taught clearly, "Whoever wishes to become great among you must be your servant, and whoever wishes to be first among you must be slave of all" (Mark 10:43-44). As we bear each others' loads, we "fulfill the law of Christ" (Gal. 6:2).

The Bible focuses on holiness of heart and life. Beginning with God's call to Abraham and continuing with the coming of Christ, God promises "to grant us that we, being rescued from the hands of our enemies, might serve him without fear, in holiness and righteousness before him all our days" (Luke 1:74-75). Peter's summons to a holy life applies to all disciples of Jesus Christ: "Be holy in all that you do just as God who called you is holy" (1 Pet. 1:15). Everything you do should move toward fulfilling that purpose. Prayer, Bible study, self-discipline, exercises in spiritual formation—and the gifts of the Spirit—are not ends, but means to an end.

Helen Keller contracted a fever at the age of nineteen months. The sickness destroyed both her hearing and sight. With the help of a dedicated teacher named Anne  Sullivan, Helen eventually learned to speak. Later in life, Miss Keller said, "Your success and happiness lie in you. External conditions are the accidents of life." The great enduring realities are love and service. God gives us spiritual gifts so we can help each other toward lives of holiness. "For God has revealed his grace for the salvation of all mankind. That grace instructs us to give up ungodly living and worldy passions, and live self-controlled, upright, and godly lives in this world" (Titus 2:11-12).

5. Every Gift Is Important

An old fable tells the story about some unhappy members of a body. The eyes, ears, hands, and feet complained that the stomach took all the food and did nothing in return. The grouchy members of the body agreed to deny the stomach any more meals. Soon, however, these disgruntled parts of the body became weak and began to starve. They recognized the stomach was essential for their well-being, and they restored their link with the stomach. Immediately, the stomach began to return nourishment to the eyes, ears, hands, and feet. Never again did the other members of the body complain against the stomach.

Christians are members of Christ's body, and the different members serve different purposes. Some ministries are public and other ministries are more fitting for individual settings. Some gifts need the use of words; others best express themselves through deeds. Some gifts lead to public praise; others bring few compliments and little applause. Yet all ministries are essential. The Bible would not support someone saying, "Because I have this gift, I'm not important." Scripture does not justify anyone saying, "Because I have this gift, I'm more important than others." God made us individually, and each of us has worth and dignity. In an orchestra the piccolo and tympani are necessary complements to the violins and violas. In God's plan, each of us needs all of us.

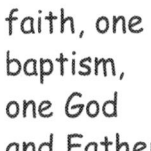

St. Paul taught, "There is one body and one Spirit, just as you were called to the one hope of your calling, one Lord, one faith, one baptism, one God and Father

of all, who is above all and through all and in all. But each of us was given grace according to the measure of Christ's gift [and] he gave gifts to his people" (Eph. 4:4-7). Christians belong to one body. And Christ is the head of that body. Each Christian has important ministries to perform. Giving to and receiving from others is as important as the parts of the human body working together in harmony.

Occasionally we hear someone say, "I can be a perfectly good Christian without being a part of the church." That view reflects a secular philosophy of human independence. The biblical view is not *independence*, but *interdependence*. We need others and others need us. Once, Dwight L. Moody and a Christian gentleman talked about participation in the church. Moody's friend said, "I can be a good Christian without ever going to church or having Christian friends." Without replying, Mr. Moody arose, removed a burning piece of wood from the fireplace, and placed it on the

hearth. The two friends watched silently as the lone log soon stopped burning.

6. God Holds Us Accountable for Discovering And Using Our Spiritual Gifts

Scripture teaches that we will answer to God for our faithful use of his gifts. After listing some of the *charismata*, St. Paul added, "Work hard and do not be lazy. Serve the Lord with a heart full of devotion" (Rom. 12:11). St. Paul wrote Timothy, "I remind you to rekindle the gift of God that is within you...for God did not give us a spirit of cowardice, but rather a spirit of power and of love and of self-discipline" (2 Tim. 1:6-7). Jesus' parable of the talents leaves no doubt that God expects us to be faithful caretakers of all that he has given us (Matt. 25:14-30). The nineteenth-century American statesman Daniel Webster said, "The most important thought I ever had was that of my individual responsibility to God."

In 1563, the Protestants in Europe created the Heidelberg Catechism. This short manual of Christian doctrine stated important Christian teachings. Question #55 asks, "What do you understand by the communion of saints?" The answer states, "Believers...have part in [the Holy Spirit] and in all his treasures and gifts.... Each one must feel himself bound to use his gifts, readily and cheerfully, for the advantage and welfare of other members." Over the years, the church may have neglected spiritual gifts. Still, their responsible use is an important part of Christianity.

Jesus said, "Much is required from the person to whom much is given" (Luke 12:48). As we use our spiritual gifts, we should become more effective as every year passes. Scripture tells us that we "must all appear before the judgment seat of Christ, so that each may receive recompense for what has been done in the body, whether good or evil" (2 Cor. 5:10). Jesus advised, "Let your light shine before others, so that they may see your good works and give glory to your Father in heaven" (Matt. 5:16).

The Holy Spirit never turns us into passive people. He always allows for our choices. We differ from inanimate objects. Lightbulbs have no choice about whether to glow when someone flips on the electric switch. Even animals act mostly from instinct, not by choices. People alone can *choose*, and we do so moment by moment. Elijah said to the ancient Israelites, "How long will you go limping with two different opinions? If the LORD is God, follow him; but if Baal, then follow him" (1 Kings 18:21).

Sometimes people will say, "The Holy Spirit possessed me in such a way that I had no control over what I was saying or what I did." I once saw the following sign in front of a church:

> "When you pass through these doors, leave your mind outside. Come to worship here only with your spirit."

This idea, however well-intentioned, is seriously misguided. We must remember that Jesus said, "'You shall love the Lord your God with all your heart, and with all your soul, and with all your mind."

The Holy Spirit always works in harmony with the human spirit. St. Paul shows the link between God's initiative and our response: "God is working in you, giving you the desire and the power to do what pleases him" (Phil. 2:13). It is biblically sound to say, *Without God we cannot, and without us God will not.*

7. The Fruit of the Spirit, Especially Love, Must Regulate Spiritual Gifts

People often point out that St. Paul placed the thirteenth chapter of 1 Corinthians (about love) between the twelfth and fourteenth chapters (about gifts). The early church at Corinth experienced all the spiritual gifts, but the congregation was immature, full of conflict, and divided. Their problems included immorality, lawsuits, and cliques. Disorder troubled their worship services, and their concern with small things buried more important matters.

St. Paul's letter to this church refers to the members as spiritual infants. The congregation boasted of its spiritual gifts, but sorely lacked the fruit of the Spirit. So to highlight the necessary balance between spiritual gifts and spiritual fruit, St. Paul apparently placed Chapter 13 in the middle of his discussion of spiritual gifts. He wrote,

> If I could speak in any language in heaven or on earth but didn't love others, I would only be making meaningless noise like a loud gong or a clanging cymbal. If I had the gift of prophecy, and if I knew all the mysteries of the future and knew everything about everything, but didn't love others, what good would I be? And if I had the gift of faith so that I could speak to a mountain and make it move, without love I would be no good to anybody. If I gave everything I have to the poor and even sacrificed my body, I could boast about it; but if I didn't love others, I would be of no value whatsoever. (NLT).

These verses reinforce the truth that one might have several gifts of the Spirit, but without love they have no more value than a noisy gong.

The fruit of the Spirit needs the gifts of the Spirit as the means of helping others. The gifts of the Spirit need the fruit of the Spirit to keep them in proper focus, regulate them, and make them Christ-like.

Summary

The seven principles in this chapter help us understand and use the spiritual gifts God gives us. Let's summarize: God gives gifts to all. He gives them apart from our deserving them. He gives them sovereignly and wisely. He gives them to enable us to serve. Every gift is important, and God holds us accountable for our stewardship of gifts. Finally, spiritual gifts must be balanced with spiritual fruit.

These principles will help direct our focus, and they lead us into the joy of serving God.

I Corinthinans 16:14

A Personal Exercise and a Group Discussion
(It is recommended that this group discussion take place before beginning Chapter 5).

Chapter 5 contains seven points that apply to your life.

Check out your thoughts about each point by marking the letter you think best fits you.

After the participants have responded to the following statements, have a group dialogue. If your group consists of more than six, it's best to have a moderator.

_____1. **All Christians have spiritual gifts.**

A. Maybe others have spiritual gifts, but I don't think I do.
B. I believe God has a spiritual gift (or gifts) for me, but I don't have any idea what mine are.
C. I think only one Christian in a thousand has any of the New Testament spiritual gifts.
D. I believe I do have at least one spiritual gift, perhaps more—and I'm eager to have God confirm them in my life.

READ 1 CORINTHIANS 12:4-10

_____2. **God gives us spiritual gifts apart from human deserving.**

A. Yes, I agree that everything we have in life comes from the grace of God.
B. No, I disagree. God gives gifts only to those who deserve them.
C. Well, I think that God meets us halfway. If we do our part, he will do his part.
D. Sometimes yes, sometimes no.

READ MATTHEW 16:18; 2 TIMOTHY 2:21; JAMES 1:17

_____3. God gives these gifts according to his perfect will.

A. I think God's will partially depends on what we want to do. I mean, how can I be happy unless I get what I want.
B. I believe God is all knowing and all wise, and I think he gives Christians the gifts that are best for them.
C. This is a subject about which we have little knowledge or understanding.
D. It depends on which denomination you belong to.

READ 1 CORINTHIANS 12:11; HEBREWS 2:4

_____4. God gives gifts for ministry and service.

A. I believe the main reason God gives us spiritual gifts is to prove that we are Christians.
B. I think God gives us spiritual gifts mostly to make us happy and joyful.
C. I believe spiritual gifts are for service and ministry to others.
D. The main reason God gives us spiritual gifts is to prove that he's awesome and powerful.

READ MARK 10:43-44; 1 CORINTHIANS 12:7; PHILIPPIANS 2:3-4; 1 PETER 4:10

_____5. Every gift is important.

A. I disagree. If the human body can survive without an arm or a leg, the church does not need each of the spiritual gifts.
B. I agree. In a healthy body all its members have an important role.
C. I don't know. Paul may have said so, but Paul may have been wrong.
D. I'm undecided. I need to know more before I make up my mind.

READ 1 CORINTHIANS 12:12-20

Directing the Focus 79

____6. **God holds us accountable for discovering and using our spiritual gifts.**

   A. I don't like the idea that God holds us accountable. He's too loving ever to judge us for what we do or don't do.
   B. We can't say Yes or No to this statement. How can I be sure?
   C. I believe the Bible teaches that we are accountable for how we live our lives.
   D. I'd rather just trust in God's love and mercy.

READ MATTHEW 25:14-30

____7. **The fruit of the Spirit, especially love, must regulate spiritual gifts.**

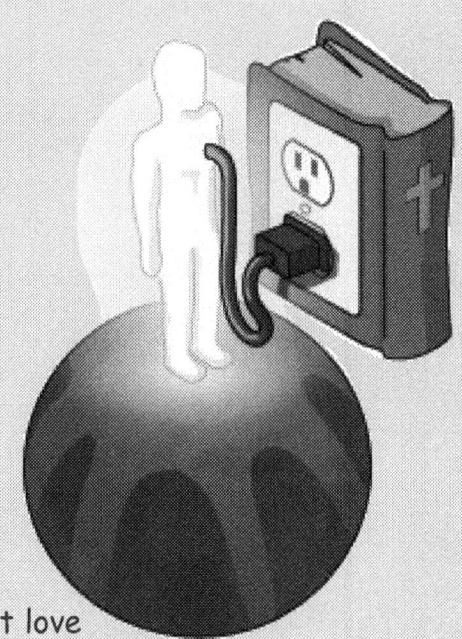

   A. If we're in the right, I don't think how we act toward others has much bearing on how faithful we are to God's truth.
   B. Whoa! Aren't spiritual gifts and the fruit of the Spirit the same thing?
   C. So long as we avoid sin, our attitudes are not important.
   D. Yes, I agree. It makes sense that love must shape the way we use our spiritual gifts.

READ I CORINTHIANS CHAPTER 13

"Order is not pressure which is imposed on society from without, but an equilibrium which is set up from within."
—Jose Ortega y Gasset (1883-1955), Spanish philosopher, university professor, and politician.

6
Discovering the Prize

This final chapter focuses on discovering your spiritual gifts. Let's look at an action plan consisting of five practical suggestions. Each one begins with a verb, an action word that is practical. Then, we'll end the book with an inventory that will help you know your spiritual gifts.

1. An Action Plan for Serious Seekers

We have seen that God did not make us passive people. The Christian life is one of active relationships—relationships between us and God, and between us and others. Of course God takes the first step toward us. After all, he created us. And, because he made us, he expects us to do something with our lives. The following suggestions point to some simple steps that will enable you to find your gifts.

1) Open yourself to God as an instrument for his use.

God reaches out to us through his revealed will in scripture and by the Holy Spirit working in our lives. Study the gifts of the Spirit and ask God to help you understand his will for you.

God is less interested in our intelligence and talents than in our willingness and obedience. He seeks not our *ability*, but our *availability*. Our proper response to God is to pray, "Lord, I do not ask for my will to be done but for yours to be done in me and through me. I give myself to you as your willing instrument for your use as you see fit. Show me what gifts you have for me, and teach me to respond to your work in my life."

(2) Examine your wishes for service and ministry.

God works within us to make us what he created us to be. His plan for us is not to reduce our joy, creativity, or fulfillment. Rather, he wants to bring us to greater levels of personal development.

Some people hold the mistaken notion that God wants us to deny all our dreams and hopes. King David had the right outlook. He wrote, "Take delight in the LORD, and he will give you the desires of your heart" (Psa. 37:4). Take seriously your visions, hopes, and ambitions. The Holy Spirit may be giving you mental pictures of his will for your life. Sanctified dreams are good, when we satisfy them God's way.

(3) Identify the most pressing needs you see in the church and the world.

Pay attention to your concerns about the world around you. Your spiritual gifts enable you to see more clearly the needs God may want you to meet.

A strong regard for unsaved people, for example, may mean that God has given you the gift of evangelism. A persistent interest in hurting, hungry, and helpless people can mean that you have the gift of helps. Think about your concerns. Your spiritual gift sensitizes your awareness of needs in the area of your gifts.

(4) Obey fully all you understand of God's will.

Jesus said, "They who have my commandments and keep them are those who love me...and I will love them and reveal myself to them" (John 14:21). Obedience to the understanding we have always leads to still greater light we do not yet have.

Suppose someone with an undiscovered gift of evangelism takes seriously Jesus' statement, "You will receive power when the Holy Spirit has come upon you; and you will be my witnesses" (Acts 1:8). By becoming a witness, that person may discover her gift of evangelism. If we respond to Christ's invitation to pray, we may find that God has given us the gift of faith. Only by obeying the command to become liberal and cheerful givers could we discover we have the gift of giving.

If we prove faithful in a little, God will increase our opportunities and rewards. A sure way to know Christ more clearly is to follow him more nearly.

(5) Evaluate the responses of other Christians.

All New Testament discussions of spiritual gifts occur with reference to the Christian community. St. Paul said, "We do not live to ourselves, and we do not die to ourselves"

(Rom. 14:7). God does not intend for us to exist as isolated hermits. The fellowship of other  Christians can confirm us in our spiritual gifts and help us see what our gifts are *not*.

I heard a man in a western state say, "I have the gift of prophecy, but no one in the congregation ever has the ability to listen to me." If others never respond favorably to you in an area of ministry, you may not have a spiritual gift for that work.

On the other hand, the positive responses of others can help confirm your spiritual gifts. God intends for us to affirm one another in the gifts he has given. You may be sure that God has greater interest in you than you have in him.

The five suggestions listed above provide a practical plan of action for discovering your spiritual gifts. *Open, examine, identify, obey,* and *evaluate*. These guidelines can help all serious seekers find the gifts God has for them.

2. An Inventory for Discovering Your Spiritual Gifts

The purpose of the following spiritual gifts inventory is to help you discover the *charismata* that God gave you. You'll be most accurate in finding out about your gifts when you respond to your interests, experiences, spiritual wishes, and how you think others see you. Avoid marking the statements based only what you think you should mark or how someone else might react to your responses. Also, don't answer positively just because you believe the statement describes "a fine thing for the church" or "a ministry that needs doing." It's important for you to mark the statements according to how they apply to you.

You need to know both what your spiritual gifts *are*, and what they *are not*. We have seen that Christians don't all have the same gifts. Obviously, God has not called all of us to the same ministries. Knowing what gifts we do not have keeps us out of trying to do the kinds of ministries we aren't fitted for; knowing what our gifts are leads us into ministries God intends for us.

There is no "right" or "wrong" answer. Just be as honest as you can.

Printed below you will find *A Spiritual Gifts Inventory*. This inventory contains 100 statements that will help you discover your spiritual gift(s). Some sentences will not fit you at all, and other statements will describe you accurately. Mark your response to each of the 100 statements on a scale from 0 to 5.

- **Zero** means that the statement does not apply to you, or that you have a negative response.
- **Five** means that the statement describes you quite well, and you have a very positive response.
- **Numbers 2, 3, and 4** fit somewhere between "Does not apply" and ""Very much applies."

When you have responded to each of the 100 statements, add up the numbers in the rows that go across the page. For instance, add together the numbers you placed after 1, 21, 41, 61, and 81. Enter your totals into the right hand column of the **Summary Sheet for Spiritual Gifts Inventory** (p. 93).

Next, enter your combined scores on page 95. That page contains a chart named **Identifying My Spiritual Gifts**. The chart contains the names of all 20 of the gifts of the Holy Spirit.

As you look over your totals, you'll see that one or more spiritual gifts have scores higher than the other spiritual gifts. One or more spiritual gifts will stand out above the others. Enter those gifts on page 96.

You might have one gift, two gifts, or three gifts. Maybe more. Every Christian has at least one spiritual gift (but no Christian has all the gifts of the Holy Spirit). You may feel surprised by  what you learn. Or, the inventory may confirm what you already believe or suspect about yourself. You have cause to thank God he's gifted you with wonderful abilities, which can shape what you do with the rest of your life.

A Spiritual Gifts Inventory©
(To the left of each statement enter 0, 1, 2, 3 4, or 5

_____1. I have a strong wish to set up a new Christian community where one does not exist. I believe I could adapt to a strange culture and talk to the people about Jesus.

_____2. I like to tell others about God's word and how it can speak to them in their daily lives.

_____3. I am deeply concerned for lost people, and I can boldly share God's love with them and invite them to give their lives to Jesus Christ.

_____4. It's as natural for me to help guide others in their Christian life as it is for a coach to develop the members of the team.

_____5. I can understand Christian truth that God shows me, and I feel an urge to teach it to others.

_____6. My greatest satisfaction is to serve the needs of others. I'd rather remain in the background than stand front and center.

_____7. I want to encourage others to follow sound counsel and become what God wants them to be.

_____8. I would rather give a gift than receive one, and I find much joy in sharing with others.

_____9. It gives me satisfaction to lead a group in a project that will benefit others.

_____10. I feel empathy for people with hurts and problems, and God helps me comfort them.

_____11. God often moves me to pray for sick people, and I believe God can heal any human hurt.

_____12. There have been times when I have prayed for something that seemed to have no solution, and God has worked miraculously.

_____13. More than once, I have spoken in tongues.

_____14. When others speak in tongues, I sometimes understand the meaning of what they say.

_____15. Sometimes God uses me to suggest a sensible course of action when others seem confused about what to do.

_____16. At times I have become aware of something good God is doing in someone's life, such as healing, saving, or blessing them.

_____17. In response to my prayers of faith, God has worked wonderfully, even when circumstances seemed insurmountable.

_____18. I have noticed false teachings in sermons or books, even when my friends sensed nothing wrong with them.

_____19. I have a special concern to help weak and needy people, and I enjoy serving them.

_____20. It's natural for me to lead others because I'm able to think about future possibilities and seek God's guidance for the group.

_____21. I long intently to see groups of people who know nothing about Christ come to know him.

_____22. Even if I never preach a sermon, I have an inner urge to tell others about the wonderful plan God has for them and how he grieves when we turn away from him.

_____23. It's easier for me than for many of my friends to talk to people about committing their lives to Jesus Christ as their Savior.

_____24. I'm concerned about the spiritual well-being and doctrinal soundness of others, and I believe I have a responsibility to help them become better disciples.

_____25. I have an inner urge to understand the Bible and to find opportunities to explain its truths to others.

_____26. I think my ministry is to serve the needs of those who minister through their teaching, preaching, and leading.

_____27. I enjoy writing notes of encouragement and helping build confidence in people to inspire them to be and do their best.

_____28. Every so often God guides me to give money to a specific need or a particular cause. Sometimes, I sense the amount he wants me to give.

_____ 29. When a project is challenging, I can organize a team to get the work done.

_____ 30. I feel compassion for people in misery, affliction, and distress, even if others say they don't deserve our sympathy.

_____ 31. I want God to make sick people whole, and I think he wants to use me as an instrument of his healing.

_____ 32. I believe God works miracles today. I've seen more than one, and I think God wants to give us incredible blessings.

_____ 33. Praying in tongues helps me get closer to God.

_____ 34. When I interpret someone who speaks in tongues, I want nonChristians to be present so they can hear the interpretation.

_____ 35. I believe God sometimes helps me to understand how the Bible speaks to confused and controversial issues.

_____ 36. Now and again, I surprise someone by telling them something about themselves that they have never told me. Sometimes, I just know.

_____ 37. I believe God has promised to do marvelous works, especially when we need him most.

_____ 38. I feel strongly agitated when people who claim divine authority teach or preach ideas contrary to scripture.

_____ 39. I'm quick to notice the practical needs of others, and I don't need credit for the menial kinds of service I can give them.

_____ 40. I have a knack for organizing, and I can lead people to work together and help them to agree on common goals and to cooperate to achieve them.

_____ 41. I think God might want me to go to people of a different culture to tell them about salvation. I wouldn't care if it were here at home or somewhere halfway around the world.

_____ 42. I am not afraid to take a strong stand for God's truth and to apply it to present circumstances.

_____ 43. I'm willing to speak openly about my faith in Christ, and I like to lead others to trust in him as their Savior.

_____44. I can be patient with people who make slow progress in their Christian lives. Even when they don't want my help, I'm willing to be there for them.

_____45. I believe it's important to test all religious teaching by scriptures, and it bothers me to hear someone distort the Christian message.

_____46. I have a greater concern for the needs of others than for my own needs.

_____47. I'm known as an encourager and one who helps sincere people get on the right track and stay on it. You might say I'm a spiritual cheerleader.

_____48. It seems that almost every time I give money to God's work or to people in need God makes ways for me to have additional money so I can give still more.

_____49. I can see the whole picture better than many others, and I can direct a group project. I don't boast about it, but I believe God made me to be a leader.

_____50. I have a strong wish to express love and caring toward helpless people who are troubled and under stress.

_____51. More than once, when I prayed for sick people God healed them.

_____52. At times, I have prayed and God has worked humanly impossible results.

_____53. I have prayed in tongues, and no one pressured me to do so or "taught" me how.

_____54. When I hear others speak in tongues, I sometimes think they are not praying to God.

_____55. Often the group turns to me for advice about a proper course of action.

_____56. More than once I have talked with someone and God has helped me to see what his or her real problem is. Sometimes they did not know it themselves until I helped them see it.

Discovering the Prize 89

_____57. It's natural for me to pray for miracles in people's lives. When I've prayed and asked God to work in mighty ways, he sometimes has.

_____58. God has helped me detect false teachings so I could warn my friends and point them in the right way.

_____59. Without anyone asking me, I often feel led to help downcast people that others neglect.

_____60. As a leader, I can see the problems of the group and take the responsibility to help the people overcome them. People trust me and accept my leadership.

_____61. I have spiritual gifts that would enable me to do pioneer missionary work among those who have never heard about Jesus Christ.

_____62. As a part of witnessing to God's wonderful word, I believe God uses me to oppose religious lies and to champion Christian truth.

_____63. I have a deep concern to see lost people come to Jesus Christ, and I feel comfortable talking with them about their need to become Christians.

_____64. It's important for me to keep confidences and to know the strengths and weakness of my Christian friends so I can encourage them along the way.

_____65. I especially enjoy hearing and reading biblically based teachings and thinking about the "what" and "why" issues.

_____66. I sometimes see ways to perform works of practical service, even when others do nothing about those needs and opportunities.

_____67. I am able to inspire others to follow good advice and start doing God's will. When they become downcast and discouraged, I can often lift them up and get them going with renewed joy.

_____68. I am keenly sensitive to the material needs of others, and I want to supply those needs out of what God has given me.

_____69. I would prefer to manage a work project to fix up a house for a homeless family than to teach a class or preach a sermon.

_____70. People in misery do not repulse me. Rather, when I meet them I am eager to find ways to help them.

_____71. I am concerned about those who suffer physical, mental, or emotional pain, and within the last several months God has impressed me to pray for a sick friend or relative.

_____72. I believe God sometimes performs wonders when we think hope is gone. I've seen the Lord work miraculously for people's benefit.

_____73. I've prayed in tongues, and I wished I knew what I was praying.

_____74. When I hear people speak in tongues I can often tell whether or not their prayers are genuine.

_____75. More than once when the group discussed a problem, the Lord has helped me to offer sound advice that relaxed tensions and opened the right course of action.

_____76. At times, without anyone telling me, God has enabled me to know something that was taking place in someone's life.

_____77. When a circumstance seems impossible, it's easy for me to believe God will answer our prayers if we pray unselfishly and in faith that he has the power to act.

_____78. I quickly notice if public speakers misinterpret or misapply scripture.

_____79. I can see ways to help the poor and helpless, and I find joy in making them feel loved and accepted.

_____80. People say I'm a leader, and I enjoy attending to details to help the group work smoothly.

_____81. I would like to find out about another culture, or even learn another language so I could take God's good news to those who are hostile to Christianity.

_____82. Because the Bible condemns vice and hypocrisy, I feel compelled to take a stand against these evils in our society.

_____83. If I had the choice, I would rather spend time helping someone trust in Christ for the first time than to do other kinds of ministries.

_____84. I feel responsible to help my friends along the right path, even if I need to correct them when they go astray.

_____85. I am dissatisfied with unclear explanations of God's truth. I want to understand it and share it with others in the clearest way possible.

_____86. I'm willing to take action to meet the physical and practical needs of others, rather than just talk about those needs.

_____87. Others often confide in me because they sense my concern and my ability to give sound, practical counsel.

_____88. I see problems that generous giving can solve, and I feel I'm responsible to use what resources God has given me to help others.

_____89. I don't mind enlisting people to join a worthy project I'm leading.

_____90. I am careful to avoid words and actions that could inflict embarrassment or pain on others.

_____91. When I see a sick or wounded child on television, I pray for God to heal them.

_____92. I believe that if we had strong faith in God he would work miraculously in the world today.

_____93. Praying in tongues is important in my life.

_____94. Although I don't speak in tongues, I can sometimes understand what someone meant when they spoke in tongues.

_____95. Others say that God has used me to give good advice about complicated matters and difficult choices.

_____96. Now and then, God has made me aware of what he is doing in the lives of others.

_____97. Even if people waver in faith, I am able to trust God's providential working and wait for him to answer our prayers in his own way and time.

_____98. I am able to sense when religious leaders rely more on themselves than on the Holy Spirit. I can also sense when a speaker is genuinely devoted to God.

_____99. One of my greatest satisfactions is to serve needy people who have little to give in return, even if they don't seem grateful.

_____100. I enjoy bringing others together as an effective team. I like to see the members contribute their special abilities and work in harmony with one another.

Summary Sheet For Spiritual Gifts Inventory

Total

1._____	21._____	41._____	61._____	81._____	A._____
2._____	22._____	42._____	62._____	82._____	B._____
3._____	23._____	43._____	63._____	83._____	C._____
4._____	24._____	44._____	64._____	84._____	D._____
5._____	25._____	45._____	65._____	85._____	E._____
6._____	26._____	46._____	66._____	86._____	F._____
7._____	27._____	47._____	67._____	87._____	G._____
8._____	28._____	48._____	68._____	88._____	H._____
9._____	29._____	49._____	69._____	89._____	I._____
10._____	30._____	50._____	70._____	90._____	J._____
11._____	31._____	51._____	71._____	91._____	K._____
12._____	32._____	52._____	72._____	92._____	L._____
13._____	33._____	53._____	73._____	93._____	M._____
14._____	34._____	54._____	74._____	94._____	N._____
15._____	35._____	55._____	75._____	95._____	O._____
16._____	36._____	56._____	76._____	96._____	P._____
17._____	37._____	57._____	77._____	97._____	Q._____
18._____	38._____	58._____	78._____	98._____	R._____
19._____	39._____	59._____	79._____	99._____	S._____
20._____	40._____	60._____	80._____	100._____	T._____

cut along this line to remove this inventory sheet

Identifying My Spiritual Gifts
(Place your totals to the left of each spiritual gift)

_____A. Apostleship

_____B. Prophecy

_____C. Evangelism

_____D. Shepherding

_____E. Teaching

_____F. Serving

_____G. Exhortation

_____H. Giving

_____I. Giving Aid

_____J. Compassion

_____K. Healing

_____L. Working Miracles

_____M. Tongues

_____N. Interp. of tongues

_____O. Word of Wisdom

_____P. Word of Knowledge

_____Q. Faith

_____R. Discernment

_____S. Helps

_____T. Administration

List your top two, three, or four spiritual gifts.

Gifts   Total Points
_____   _____
_____   _____
_____   _____
_____   _____

After you have discovered your spiritual gift(s), you'll want to develop and deploy them. As we use our gifts to serve God and others, we will bear fruit that will last. Jesus said, "My Father is glorified by this, that you bear much fruit….I have said these things to you so my joy may be in you, and that your joy may be complete" (John 15:11).

Without God and the mighty works he does in and through us, our lives are deficient. With him, we're on our way to becoming all that God intended us to be when he first breathed us into life.

It's time to make some decisions!

Here are ten questions you can answer with **Yes** or **No**

_____1. I have at least one spiritual gift.

_____2. I'm eager to learn more about my gifts so I can develop and use them.

_____3. I'm willing to find more time to get closer to God and to begin to minister.

_____4. If I need to sacrifice in some way, I'm eager to do it so long as God is leading me.

_____5. I will begin to talk to God regularly and tell him I'm willing to do whatever he leads me to do.

_____6. I know we do not earn salvation by good works, but I believe God will someday reward his faithful servants.

_____7. I can honestly say it's less important for me to have my way with God than for God to have his way with me.

_____8. I don't always understand immediately why God allows some events to happen, but I'm willing to trust God's heart, when I cannot trace God's hand.

_____9. I'm willing to pray, "God, do anything in me today that you must, so tomorrow you can do everything through me that you plan."

_____10. Even if there are some things that seem unclear to me, in this very moment I surrender all I understand about myself to God. More than anything else, I want to be entirely his.

If you marked No to even one of these statements, you would do well to reconsider. God can bless you entirely only when you give yourself to him totally. Remember, God loves you unconditionally, and he plans a life for you infinitely better than anything you can imagine.

If you marked Yes to all ten statements, you have a future finer than your greatest dreams. In the last book of the Bible, St. John tells about a vision God gave him. This vision is about the future of those whose God is the Lord:

> I saw a new heaven and a new earth, for the first heaven and the first earth had passed away, and there was no longer any sea. I saw the Holy City, the new Jerusalem, coming down out of heaven from God, prepared as a bride beautifully dressed for her husband. And I heard a loud voice from the throne saying, 'Now the dwelling of God is with humankind, and he will live with them. They will be his people, and God himself will be with them and be their God. He will wipe every tear from their eyes. There will be no more death or mourning or crying or pain, for the old order of things has passed away.'
>
> He who was seated on the throne said, 'I am making everything new!' Then he said, 'Write this down, for these words are trustworthy and true.' He said to me: 'It is done. I am the Alpha and the Omega, the Beginning and the End. To him who is thirsty I will give to drink without cost from the spring of the water of life. He who overcomes will inherit all this, and I will be his God and he will be my child' (Rev. 21:1-7).

A Good Motto for the rest of my life

"Do all the good you can,
By all the means you can,
In all the ways you can,
In all the places you can,
At all the times you can,
To all the people you can,
As long as ever you can."
—John Wesley

John Wesley
(Drawing by Richard Douglas)

About the Author

Ken Kinghorn teaches Church History at Asbury Theological Seminary. He received his M.Div. from Asbury Theological Seminary, his Ph.D. from Emory University, and he also did postdoctoral work at Columbia University and the University of Cambridge. As well as teaching seminary classes, Ken speaks in local churches and at conference events. His speaking assignments have taken him to England, Japan, Korea, Belgium, Switzerland, Israel, Greece, and Turkey.

Ken and his wife, Hilda, have four adult children, each of whom serves in some form of Christian ministry. Ken has written 17 books, several of which have gone into such languages as Japanese, Russian, Spanish, Swedish, and Estonian. He enjoys collecting portraits and engravings of John and Charles Wesley. One of his favorite hobbies is visiting centuries-old cathedrals and churches in England and elsewhere. Ken loves gardening, woodworking, classical music, museums, and ministering in other countries beyond the U.S.A.

www.ingramcontent.com/pod-product-compliance
Lightning Source LLC
Chambersburg PA
CBHW081258170426
43198CB00017B/2832